ACHIEVING
OUTSTANDING
on your **TEACHING PLACEMENT**

Education at SAGE

SAGE is a leading international publisher of journals, books, and electronic media for academic, educational, and professional markets.

Our education publishing includes:

- accessible and comprehensive texts for aspiring education professionals and practitioners looking to further their careers through continuing professional development

- inspirational advice and guidance for the classroom

- authoritative state of the art reference from the leading authors in the field

Find out more at: **www.sagepub.co.uk/education**

JONATHAN **GLAZZARD**
and JANE **STOKOE**

ACHIEVING OUTSTANDING
on your **TEACHING PLACEMENT**

Early Years and Primary School-based Training

Los Angeles | London | New De
Singapore | Washington C

First published 2011

SAGE Publications Ltd
1 Oliver's Yard
55 City Road
London EC1Y 1SP

SAGE Publications Inc.
2455 Teller Road
Thousand Oaks, California 91320

SAGE Publications India Pvt Ltd
B 1/I 1 Mohan Cooperative Industrial Area
Mathura Road
New Delhi 110 044

SAGE Publications Asia-Pacific Pte Ltd
33 Pekin Street #02-01
Far East Square
Singapore 048763

Library of Congress Control Number: 2011922275

British Library Cataloguing in Publication data

A catalogue record for this book is available from the British Library

ISBN 978-0-85702-526-5
ISBN 978-0-85702-527-2 (pbk)

Typeset by C&M Digitals (P) Ltd, Chennai, India
Printed by MPG Books Group, Bodmin, Cornwall
Printed on paper from sustainable resources

Contents

Acknowledgements

We would like to thank all past and present students, whose experiences we have drawn on to produce this text.

Thanks are also extended to Richard Myers and Lehan Medlock who have kindly contributed to this text by providing case studies.

About the authors

Jonathan Glazzard

Jonathan has been responsible for primary Initial Teacher Training at the University of Huddersfield for the past six years. He also leads the MA in Early Years and Primary Education. Prior to his work at the university, Jonathan worked as a teacher and assistant head teacher in primary schools for ten years. He is currently engaged in research in the field of inclusive education and pupils' views of primary education.

Jane Stokoe

Jane works as an assistant head teacher in a Barnsley primary school. She has responsibility for the Early Years Foundation Stage and Key Stage 1 and also teaches children aged 4 to 6 years. Jane also leads Special Educational Needs and Inclusion within her school and works in partnership with the University of Huddersfield to support trainee teachers, both as a link tutor and as a senior mentor. In working with trainees, Jane is able to share her expertise with them but also enjoys learning from them. She has taught for 35 years and continues to enjoy the many challenges and rewards presented to her in her chosen profession.

Table of acronyms

APP   Assessing Pupils' Progress

ARG   Assessment Reform Group

ASD   Autistic Spectrum Disorder

AST   Advanced Skills Teacher

CPD   Continuing Professional Development

DfES   Department for Education and Skills

EPPE   Effective Provision of Pre-School Education

EYFS   Early Years Foundation Stage

ICT   Information Communication Technology

INSET   In-Service Training

ITT   Initial Teacher Training

KS1   Key Stage 1

NQT   Newly Qualified Teacher

Ofsted   Office for Standards in Education

QCA   Qualifications and Curriculum Authority

QTS   Qualified Teacher Status

REPEY   Researching Effective Pedagogy in the Early Years

ZPD   Zone of Proximal Development

Glossary of key terms

Achievement
Achievement refers to a measure of a child's knowledge, skills and understanding at a given point in time.

Assessment for learning
'The process of seeking and interpreting evidence for use by learners and their teacher to decide where the learners are in their learning, where they need to go and how best to get there' (Assessment Reform Group, 2002).

Attainment
Attainment refers to a measurement of children's knowledge, skills and understanding at a fixed point in time against national age-related expectations.

Auditory learners
Auditory learners predominantly learn through listening. These learners will learn effectively through listening to adults and peers in either whole-class or group situations.

Community cohesion
According to Alan Johnson:

> By community cohesion, we mean working towards a society in which there is a **common vision** and **sense of belonging** by all communities; a society in which the diversity of people's backgrounds and circumstances is appreciated and valued; a society in which similar **life opportunities** are available to all; and a society in which strong and positive relationships exist and continue to be developed in the workplace, in schools and in the wider community. (Alan Johnson, Secretary of State for Education and Skills, speaking in Parliament on 2 November 2006. Based on the Government and the Local Government Association's definition first published in Guidance on Community Cohesion, LGA, 2002 and resulting from the Cantle Report in 2001.)

Creativity

According to Hayes, 'In short, creative learning necessitates a clearly formulated lesson structure, within which opportunities for pupils to reflect, think and be innovative can mature and enlarge, supported by a language-rich environment' (2009: 14). Creative teachers:

> allow children to be creative and do not restrict their ideas;
> allow children to use their imagination in a range of ways;
> develop a creative classroom which is resourceful, colourful, inspiring, imaginative and exciting so that pupils want to learn;
> promote learning through first-hand experiences and outdoor education;
> create imaginative contexts for learning so that pupils are 'fired-up' and eager to learn;
> demonstrate connections between areas of learning, perhaps through the use of a thematic approach to curriculum organisation;
> provide opportunities for children to apply skills and knowledge through the use of enterprise projects, play-based learning and enquiry-based learning;
> provide children with opportunities to take responsibility for their own independent learning.

This is not an exhaustive list and you will be able to generate further ideas of your own.

External agencies

Colleagues from external agencies work in collaboration with school-based staff and parents and carers to support the specific needs of identified children. These children may have special educational needs or may be vulnerable. External colleagues may work for education, health or social services.

Formative assessment

This is assessment for learning. It is usually informal and based on observation or samples of work. Its purpose is to inform the ongoing process of teaching and learning and to identify children's achievements, learning needs and next steps. It informs the planning process and helps to identify focused next steps in learning. It can take place within a lesson or at the end of a lesson. Formative assessment evidence may be collected from planned or incidental opportunities.

Higher level teaching assistant

This status provides formal recognition for staff in schools that carry out an enhanced role in supporting learning and teaching. Formal recognition of this status is dependent on the demonstration of specific competencies in relation to set standards. According to Hayes higher level teaching assistants are expected to contribute to 'the full range of teaching and learning activities' (2009: 48), such as:

> planning, preparing and organising lessons;
> contributing to the assessment of pupils' learning;
> working with individuals, groups and whole classes independently.

Identity

The word 'identity' in teaching is often used to refer to a person's professional identity. Professional identity is shaped by a person's own philosophical position and the ownership of a set of guiding principles, values and beliefs which ultimately shape personal practice.

Initial Professional Development

Initial Professional Development (IPD) refers to a planned programme of training to meet the specific needs of trainee teachers during periods of school-based and centre-based ITT. This includes:

> the identification of trainees' targets on an action plan or individual training plan;
> a planned programme of activities to address these specific targets including tutorials with academic tutors or school mentors, observing teachers in other classrooms, meeting subject leaders or staff with specific responsibilities, visiting other schools, personal research and engagement with on-line communities or subject specialist associations (not an exhaustive list);
> reflection following periods of IPD activity on the personal learning and development that has taken place and the identification of future learning needs.

Kinaesthetic learners

These learners tend to learn effectively through first-hand experiences. They enjoy practical tasks and learning through concrete experiences. They may prefer to be more active than passive.

Lateral thinkers

Lateral thinking is a term originally used by Edward de Bono. Lateral thinking involves solving problems through an indirect and creative approach. It is about reasoning that is not immediately obvious and the application of new approaches to thinking and problem solving.

Learning objectives

Learning objectives are statements of intent related to learning. They describe the knowledge, skills and understanding that the teacher wishes to develop during the course of a lesson. Learning objectives (often referred to as 'Programmes of Study') are identified in the National Curriculum (DfEE, 1999) and the EYFS framework (DfES, 2007) (in this document they are referred to as 'Development Matters'). They are often broad in scope and may need to be broken down into smaller steps.

Learning outcomes

These are focused statements which communicate clearly how learners can demonstrate success at the end of a lesson or unit of work. They should be written in a child-friendly manner. Additionally they should be differentiated to enable learners at different stages of development to demonstrate their learning and to enable teachers and children to recognise their successes in learning. They should be framed using positive language, for example: *I can say the number that is one more than a number between 1 and 9*. They should be measurable and support the child in evaluating their own learning as well as enabling the teacher to plan for next steps in learning.

Medium-term planning

Medium-term plans provide an overview of a teaching sequence within a subject, area of learning or theme. These plans outline the intended coverage of specific learning objectives across a sequence of lessons and they may provide an outline of intended teaching activities and intended learning outcomes.

Multi-agency

Multi-agency working refers to a group of professionals who work together and in partnership with parents, carers or the child to enable the child to achieve the best possible outcomes. A multi-agency team may include professionals from education, health and social services. In many instances these teams support vulnerable learners or learners with additional needs.

On-line communities

An on-line community refers to a group of people with similar interests who sub-scribe to a specific organisation/website. Through the use of discussion boards, blogs and other web-based tools, members of these communities can exchange ideas and resources. These communities are excellent vehicles for facilitating the development of reflective practice.

Parent partnership

Parent partnership is a broad concept and includes:

> listening to the voice of the parent(s) or carer(s) when expressing views on all aspects of their child's education and care;
> genuine partnership working which embraces the notion of parents and professionals working together to raise outcomes for all children.

Personalised provision

Personalised provision refers to educational provision which specifically meets the individual needs of learners. Effective personalised provision takes into account the intellectual, social, emotional and physical needs of learners and is therefore child centred. It also takes into consideration the individual interests and viewpoints of learners.

Professional

Behaving as a professional is important in teaching. This relates to adhering to the rules and expectations of a range of stakeholders, including parents, col-leagues, pupils and society as a whole, so that you do not bring the profession into disrepute. Your own ITT provider will have a Code of Professional Conduct which will intimately guide your practice.

Professional learning community

A professional learning community refers to a group of people within an organisation who work together in a collaborative way to meet specific identi-fied goals. Such communities embrace team working and the exchange of ideas and are united in a common purpose. Within a school the professional learning community includes all staff, parents, carers, pupils, governors and staff from external agencies.

Progress

Progress refers to the measurement of learning that has taken place between two fixed points in time. It takes into account the child's starting point and level of achievement and represents an evaluation of the learning which has taken place between the two points.

Pupil voice

Pupil voice refers to the processes of seeking the views of learners, listening to what learners have to say and acting upon those views. The notion of learner voice views learners as active agents, who are capable of making decisions and taking responsibility for their own learning. Through being given opportunities to express their views pupils are viewed as equal participants within the learning process. The use of pupil voice affects the balance of power within schools; in schools that embrace pupil voice, power is distributed between learners and educators.

Scaffolding

The term 'scaffolding' refers to the process of supporting a learner to reach a higher level of development. Children usually make better progress and achieve their potential when they are supported in the learning process. A practitioner can scaffold a child's learning through the use of modelling, questioning, demonstration or explanation. This is particularly effective when children have a specific misconception and through scaffolding, adults can support learners through this. Eventually the child will master the learning independently and will no longer need the support. At this point the child has reached a higher level of understanding and moved through their ZPD (see below). Scaffolding can also be used between learners and this is particularly effective when children at higher stages of development support children at lower stages of development. An application of this strategy is the use of 'talk partners'.

Short-term planning

Short-term planning refers to day-to-day lesson planning or weekly plans. It is developed on the basis of prior assessments of the needs of learners.

Socio-cultural theory

Socio-cultural theory emphasises the importance of children learning through social interaction and first-hand experiences. It stresses the role of language within the learning process and recognises that learning is mediated through social and cultural values.

Statement of special educational needs

A statement of special educational needs refers to the formal recognition by the local authority that a child has specific additional needs. The statement is an official document which identifies the specific needs of the learner and ways that these needs should be addressed.

Subject knowledge

Subject knowledge for trainee teachers includes pedagogical knowledge (i.e. the knowledge of how to teach a subject effectively and how to develop effective pedagogical approaches for curriculum delivery and organisation for specific subjects and age phases) and subject knowledge per se (which refers to your own level of knowledge and understanding of the skills, knowledge and concepts within specific subjects).

Subject specialist associations

Subject specialist associations have been established to provide educators with a wealth of information in relation to best practice within specific subjects. The organisations share resources, pedagogical knowledge and research with their members and thus such organisations facilitate the process of reflection. Many of these organisations operate through websites, but this may be supplemented through the use of regular journals, CPD courses or conferences. Case studies of best practice or practitioner action research are often shared with members of such organisations.

Success criteria

Success criteria are often referred to as 'learning outcomes'. (See the definition of this term.)

Summative assessment

This is the assessment of learning and takes place at a fixed point in time. It provides a summary of the child's attainment at the end of a unit of work, a term, a year or a key stage. It may be formal but the judgement can also be based on continuous assessment of the child's learning over the given period of time. The outcomes may be communicated to parents or the local authority, for example statutory assessment tests or Foundation Stage profile scores at the end of the EYFS.

Visual learners

Visual learners thrive in learning contexts that make good use of visual imagery. These learners can often make sense of learning when information is presented in pictures, diagrams, models and through digital images. This is not an exhaustive list.

Zone of proximal development

The zone of proximal development (ZPD), introduced by Vygotsky (1978), refers to the distance between a learner's actual level of development and their potential development. Learners can move from one point to another through the support and guidance of more able adults or peers. Teaching is most effective when it is pitched within this zone.

Introduction

At the time of this book going into production the education system in England is in a state of transition. The government has set out its vision for schools and ITT in its White Paper: *The Importance of Teaching: The Schools White Paper 2010* (DfE, 2010). The document contains clear messages about the need to reform ITT, the curriculum in schools and assessment processes.

In the future more emphasis will be placed on school-based training with trainees spending a greater proportion of their time in schools. In addition, training places will be offered to graduates with the best degrees and there will be a stronger focus on faster routes into teaching for graduates from good universities. Exciting programmes such as *Teach First* will be expanded and additional short training programmes will be introduced, with a view to attracting the most able graduates into the profession. The White Paper emphasises that teacher training must include a stronger focus on reading, mathematics and behaviour management. The future of university ITT routes remains uncertain and concerns have been expressed from the academic community about the new emphasis on the training of teachers as opposed to the education of teachers.

In schools, the White Paper emphasises that teachers and head teachers will have greater powers with respect to pupil discipline. There will be a strong focus on the core subjects and the curriculum will be reviewed and non-essential elements will be removed. The assessment system will be reformed and accountability will be increased. The government also plans to ensure that all young people participate in education or training up to the age of 18 by 2015. The government has stressed its commitment to the National Curriculum and a review of the existing National Curriculum has been launched. At the time of going to print the government is reviewing the EYFS and there is uncertainty within this sector about the current framework and assessment processes for children in the birth to 5 age range.

It is clear that those of us in the education community are living in times of change and uncertainty. We are in a state of transition. It is difficult to predict precisely what the future holds. At the time of writing the policies and curriculum frameworks stated in this text are current. The websites listed at the end of chapters are live and the criteria identified by Ofsted for grading trainees are taken from the current inspection framework for ITT. We are aware that policy will change over the next few months and years and that it will be necessary to update this text in light of this. However, we believe that this text will still be a valuable resource for trainee teachers.

Each chapter includes practical strategies which trainee teachers can consider to support them during periods of school-based ITT. Examples are illustrated through case studies and there are opportunities for trainees to reflect on these throughout the text. The book is organised in relation to the current standards for ITT. However, we are aware that the current professional standards will be reviewed and may be replaced by new standards which have a stronger focus on subject knowledge. The Appendix shows which standards are referred to in which chapters. Links to theories and research are made throughout the chapters. The text does not have to be read sequentially, and chapters can be read in isolation.

We hope that we have produced a text which is both practical and accessible. We also hope that we have succeeded in our original aim, which was to deconstruct the Ofsted criteria for grading trainee performance, by illustrating ways in which trainee teachers can achieve the highest outcomes by the end of their professional training. The ideas and suggestions in this text are based on our years of experience as primary school teachers and teacher educators.

1

Professional attributes

This chapter covers

Ofsted (2009) has identified several noticeable characteristics of 'outstanding' trainee teachers. This chapter examines each of these characteristics in turn. Each characteristic is exemplified to enable trainee teachers to identify whether they are demonstrating them during periods of school-based placement. The chapter focuses heavily on how trainees can develop creative, innovative approaches in teaching. It addresses the notion of being a risk taker and it stresses the importance of a flexible approach.

According to Ofsted outstanding trainees:

> take risks when trying to make teaching interesting, are able to deal with the unexpected and 'grab the moment';
> inspire and communicate their enthusiasm to learners;
> have an intrinsic passion for learning;
> show innovation and creative thinking – lateral thinkers;
> have the ability to reflect critically and rigorously on their own practice to inform their professional development, and to take and evaluate appropriate actions – they are able to learn from their mistakes;
> take full responsibility for their own professional development;
> are highly respected by learners and colleagues and, where appropriate, parents/carers and employers;
> have the clear capacity to become outstanding teachers;
> demonstrate, or show the capacity to develop, leadership and management skills (2009: 36).

These characteristics will now be examined in turn to enable you to evaluate whether you are demonstrating them fully during your periods of school-based training.

Taking risks

According to Ofsted outstanding trainees 'take risks when trying to make teaching interesting, are able to deal with the unexpected and "grab the moment"' (2009: 36). However, the notion of risk is subjective and one person's perception of risk may differ radically from that of another. Consequently you may feel that you have taken a risk in your teaching but your mentor may not share this view. An example of this is illustrated through the following case study.

Case study

A trainee teacher with a Year 4 class supported the children in applying their mathematical understanding of area by engaging the children in an outdoor lesson. The children were asked to calculate the area of the football pitch. The trainee felt that the lesson was an example of risk taking and evidence of creative practice. In the post-lesson feedback tutorial the class mentor explained to the trainee that there is an expectation that children should work both inside and outside the classroom. Working outside was also common practice for this group of learners. For these reasons the mentor felt that no risks in teaching had been taken.

Reflection

> Can you think of ways in which the trainee could have genuinely taken risks to teach this aspect of mathematics?
> Reflect on lessons you have taught where you have 'played it safe'. How would you change these lessons to become a risk taker?

Being a risk taker is potentially problematic and trainees may be tempted to 'play it safe' when planning and teaching lessons. Trainees (and teachers) often mentally rehearse worst case scenarios at the planning stage and this may prevent them from taking a risk. Such scenarios include:

> learning outcomes not being met;
> the children becoming over-excited resulting in a noisy learning environment and loss of focus;
> other teachers in school not liking your teaching style.

These potential pitfalls may prevent you from taking risks in your teaching. Additionally the context you are working in will ultimately determine whether you are able to take risks in your lessons. If you are working with creative, energetic teachers who also take risks in their teaching then you will ultimately be more inclined to do the same. Unfortunately if you are placed in a school with teachers who 'play it safe' and expect you to teach in a similar way then the opportunities to take risks will be more limited. Your class mentor will play a pivotal role in this respect. If your class mentor is open to fresh ideas and approaches and regularly experiments in teaching, you are likely to model this approach.

However, we emphasise that you should be willing to experiment with teaching styles and approaches regardless of the context in which you are placed. Your ITT provider does not expect you to be a carbon copy of your class teacher. The aim of teacher training is to empower you to develop your own professional identity as a beginning teacher. By the end of your training it is important that you have formulated your own set of principles about education in general and children's learning specifically. Trainees should consequently take every opportunity to learn from experimentation, try out new ideas and evaluate their actions during periods of school-based training. Research has suggested that creative teachers frequently take risks in both their private and professional lives (Boden, 2001; Craft, 2001) so it appears that creativity and risk taking go hand in hand.

Before taking risks you need to think through carefully how you will manage the lesson if things do not go according to plan. Risk taking, by its very nature, means that children's responses and outcomes cannot always be predicted. Sometimes it is too easy to adopt a predictable structure that you know will work because you have used it many times before. Being a risk taker assumes a degree of flexibility to deviate from tried and tested structures.

Sometimes risk taking demands the flexibility to deviate from prescribed lesson planning both within and between lessons in response to what children say and do. It is not always necessary or even desirable to have each day precisely mapped out to five-minute intervals. Children come to school with new experiences each day. They bring in objects which they have either found or been given. Risk takers are able to 'grab the moment' and seize the opportunity to embrace children's interests or experiences and build these into learning experiences. Consequently risk takers are able to think on their feet.

During centre-based training you will have been introduced to specific ways of structuring lessons, particularly in literacy and mathematics. You may also have been introduced to some of the materials produced by the National Strategies. Trainees often find it helpful to follow this non-statutory guidance as it provides them with a structure upon which to base their teaching. However, there is a danger that over-prescription can stifle imagination within teaching. Trainees who take risks are willing to try out new approaches that they have never used before. They are keen to experiment with creative approaches and deviate from common approaches to structuring lessons. These trainees realise the potential benefits of varying their teaching styles in order to maximise learner participation. Cremin (2009) argues that creative teachers take ownership of planning, teaching and assessment and exert a strong sense of professional autonomy in the classroom.

Lesson stimuli

A creative stimulus for a lesson will engage and excite your learners. Think carefully about the use of the following as resources to stimulate learning:

> music;
> a piece of art work;
> a poster;
> objects from the natural work, for example bird's nest;
> a 'magic' mobile telephone;
> a rusty key;
> a letter in a bottle;
> an old boot;
> an old diary;
> a sealed box;
> a feely bag.

Consider the ways in which you may use these resources to support learning across the curriculum. Also reflect on what additional resources can support creative practices.

Trainees may be empowered by discovering that specific lessons do not have to follow specific formats. It is not necessary to start every mathematics lesson with a mental/oral starter, followed by whole-class input, focused group work and a plenary. Literacy lessons do not necessarily have to begin with a big book or a shared writing activity. Phonics lessons do not always have to follow a four-part structure. These approaches may work some of the time but if they are over-used there is a danger that the predictable structure may cause children to disengage. Varying your approach adds interest for both you and your learners.

You might decide to teach children about mathematical concepts though a series of outdoor games. A lesson of fractions can be brought to life by asking the children to make sandwiches and find different ways of cutting them into halves or quarters. A treasure hunt around the school can be an exciting way of teaching the children about logical thinking and can focus on specific areas of the curriculum. History lessons can be brought to life through the use of drama strategies. The National Strategies provide a comprehensive overview of a range of drama and speaking and listening strategies. The use of drama and talk across the whole curriculum can be a powerful and engaging way of teaching children subject-specific skills or aspects of knowledge. Trainees who take risks exploit such possibilities and use the broader curriculum as a context for applying children's literacy, numeracy and ICT skills. This approach ensures that these fundamental skills are applied and practised in context.

In all of these approaches the key point is that you firstly need to establish the intended learning outcomes. Once you are clear about what you want the children to learn you can then plan imaginative activities which address these. The intended learning outcomes should be derived from your assessments of children's prior learning. You should avoid the temptation to think of exciting activities first then match learning outcomes to fit the activity. This approach may be detrimental to children's learning, as an accurate understanding of children's misconceptions and next steps in learning should drive planning and teaching. You should therefore make sure that teaching is driven by an accurate identification of children's needs rather than being activity driven.

Practical task

You are teaching a lesson on position in mathematics to a Year 1 class. The learning objective is:

> To visualise and use everyday language to describe the position of objects.

Think of creative ways of teaching this objective. Try to make the learning active and fun.

Then take other objectives from the National Curriculum or the EYFS framework and think of innovative approaches to teach them.

Trainees who take risks recognise the value of enquiry-based learning. Fundamentally children need to be independent learners. They need to discover new learning for themselves and develop the skills needed to become lifelong learners. Passive learning and didactic approaches (imparting knowledge) have little value in today's schools. Children will quickly forget what they have been told but will remember what they have discovered for themselves. Trainees who take risks will therefore provide opportunities for their learners to practise being scientists, historians, mathematicians and so on. These trainees provide learners with opportunities to use source material to answer questions, to problem solve, experiment and research new learning. This changes the role of the teacher from someone who imparts knowledge to someone who is a facilitator of learning. The key skill in this respect is the ability to provide children with an effective learning environment, which includes the necessary resources to enable children to be independent learners. Clearly there are risks associated with such approaches but the potential benefits outweigh these. Such benefits include learner motivation and participation, opportunities for learning how to learn, and deep learning which is fostered through self-discovery.

According to Hayes:

> In a vibrant learning community, pupils not only need relevant work but also a productive engagement with thinking and problem-solving that will equip them with the skills of self-reliance when adult support is unavailable and they have to rely more on their initiative. (2009: 30)

Therefore the aim of education is to teach children to be self-sufficient and ultimately to be independent learners themselves. Outstanding teachers (and trainees) are able to facilitate children's independence by providing them with ownership of their own learning. Piaget emphasised the value of active learning and children's interaction with the physical environment. He stressed the importance of the child's involvement in their learning and the need for children to construct their own understandings (Whitebread, 2003). Vygotsky emphasised the role of social interaction and language in the learning process. Practice should be underpinned with a secure knowledge of theory so that you know why you are adopting particular approaches. Both theories have implications for teaching, and enquiry-based learning and collaborative work are good examples of approaches which reflect these theories.

Clearly children will need to be taught the necessary pre-requisite skills to enable them to get maximum benefit from independent enquiry-based learning. Without such underpinning skills (i.e. the ability to read for meaning, write, use ICT, ask questions) children will be unable to find out their own information in history, geography, religious education or citizenship. Unless children can plan an investigation, predict outcomes, control variables, identify fair testing, observe, record and draw conclusions, they will find it difficult to work as scientists. Therefore in the early years teachers have to devote a substantial amount of time to teaching specific skills. However, it is still possible to plan opportunities for independent learning in the early years through creating effective learning environments which encourage children to be curious, problem solve and apply what they have been taught.

In the early years trainees who take risks might use the children's interests as a starting point for planning and they might develop learning spaces in classrooms which reflect these interests. Involving children in the planning process is becoming increasingly common in the early years and primary age phases and consulting children regularly about what they want to learn is now seen to be good practice.

Risk taking necessitates a willingness to deviate from traditional prescribed structures to lessons. It is associated with a desire to experiment with teaching styles and approaches. Being a risk taker represents a commitment to continual experimentation and reflection. Confident trainees who take risks are not afraid to be flexible in their approaches and frequently empower children to lead the learning. Risk takers are confident practitioners who are able to build on firm foundations. They reflect and experiment and find innovative approaches to teaching and learning. In the early stages of your development you may not have the confidence to do this and time needs to be spent on establishing secure pedagogical knowledge, skills and understanding. As you gain in confidence you will be able to gradually reflect on your practice and experiment with it. However, it may be detrimental to your development to take risks too soon.

Grabbing the moment

The Ofsted criteria for evaluating trainee performance emphasise that outstanding trainee teachers are able to 'grab the moment' by capitalising on unforeseen opportunities and situations for the benefit of their learners. It is therefore important to recognise that you need to be flexible in your approach.

Flexibility is essential and trainees who demonstrate this are able to seize unplanned opportunities and integrate them into their teaching. However, this is not always easy to do. You should have planned your lessons in sufficient detail so that there is no wasted time during the day. You will be required to identify timings on your lesson plans so that your lessons can progress at a good pace. You will have identified learning objectives that must be covered and you will have specified learning outcomes for groups of learners and individuals. Additionally you may be in a school where the head teacher asks for your planning in advance and a weekly timetable. The head teacher may expect you to be teaching specific things at certain times and if you deviate from your planning then you may be required to justify this. Your university or provider link tutor will arrange visits to observe you and they may expect to see specific lessons. It is difficult to deviate from such a tightly planned schedule and your daily timetable and lesson timings may well provide you with a degree of security that you value. You have specified the schedule and you expect your learners to be at a certain stage by a specific time. You know how far you want them to progress by the end of the week as this has been specified in your weekly planning and you have identified precisely what you want them to learn.

Being flexible within this context is certainly a challenge but flexibility enables you to:

> respond to children's immediate interests;
> respond to things that children say and do either directly or in their play;
> respond to comments by parents and carers;
> respond to changes in weather, for example a sudden fall of snow;
> respond to sudden rare events, such as an earthquake;
> respond to experiences outside of education which children discuss in school, such as a family holiday/visit, cultural festival or other positive and negative experiences.

Many young children demonstrate sheer delight when there is a sudden change in the weather. If it suddenly starts to snow during the day the children's attention will immediately switch to the snow. Creative teachers can seize this opportunity and quickly adapt their lessons 'on the spot'. Thus, the theme of 'snow' can become a rich context for children's writing (both fiction and non-fiction), reading and understanding of science. Young children could investigate the properties of snow either through exploration in the outdoor area or in the classroom. Knowledgeable trainees can then observe children working with the snow and use this context as a vehicle for extending their language by introducing them to new vocabulary.

Sudden world or local events such as earthquakes, floods or hurricanes can form a stimulating context for learning across the breadth of the curriculum. Older children can research into these physical changes using enquiry-based learning approaches. They can use books and e-learning to research into specific topics and they can present the information to their peers. They can organise events to raise money for victims and use the skills associated with enterprise education to help others in situations of crisis. Such events can provide rich contexts for the development of children's writing and reading.

Children may come to school with special objects that they want to share with you and the rest of the class. These may be interesting and unusual and could potentially provide rich contexts for learning. We have worked with children over the years who have turned up with various objects. One child turned up with an old dusty boot that he found on the beach at the weekend. This raised several interesting questions:

> What was it?
> Where was it found and how did it get there?
> Who might have owned it?
> What might have happened to the owner?

This created a rich context for writing. The children decided that the boot belonged to a giant and subsequently wrote stories about how the giant lost his boot! Interesting and unusual objects can form the stimulus for a class discussion and can be displayed in the writing area in early years settings to provide a stimulus for children's writing.

 Case study

Nosheen was placed in a large EYFS unit for her first placement. The parents and carers came into the setting in the morning to meet and greet the practitioners and relationships were positive. Nosheen chatted informally to one of the fathers one morning about his child's progress. She found out that he was called Pete and that he worked for the organisation Dogs for the Blind. As a dog trainer, Pete was responsible for ensuring that the dogs were well trained for their future role.

Nosheen asked Pete if he would come into the setting to talk to the children about the organisation and his role. Pete was happy to oblige and arranged to come in the next day. He brought with him some photographs of the dog trainers and the dogs and these were displayed on the interactive whiteboard. Pete also brought some video footage to show the children a typical training session and some further footage of the dogs working with their owners.

(Continued)

(Continued)

Nosheen prepared the children for Pete's session by directing them to think of (and write down) specific questions that they wanted to ask him. The children responded really well to the session. They were engaged and asked many questions. This session then provided a context for subsequent learning in the setting over several days.

Reflection

> How did Nosheen 'grab the moment' and why was this beneficial to her learners?
> Look at the EYFS framework. What learning opportunities were presented in this session?
> What subsequent learning could you develop from this session? Refer to the EYFS framework.

If parents or carers offer to come into school to talk to the children about unusual jobs that they do then it is important to capitalise on this. One parent of a child in my class worked as a radiographer. She volunteered to come into school to show the children some X-rays. This offer was immediately taken up and she brought in a selection of interesting X-rays and a light box. Some of the X-rays showed images of lungs that were damaged by smoking. Others showed broken limbs or limbs held together by screws. The children were very engaged during the session and it would have been difficult to replicate the experience.

Parents or carers may offer to come into school to work with small groups of children. They may have a specific skill/talent that they are willing to share. Trainees who grab the moment seize these opportunities because they believe that the experience will not only be enriching but difficult to replicate. On this basis the experience is deemed to be educationally worthwhile, regardless of whether it fits in with a class topic or theme.

Trainees who grab the moment build on children's home experiences and take every opportunity to develop in their learners an appreciation of social and cultural diversity. Children within a class have diverse experiences out of school. They may attend weddings, visit other countries or take part in celebrations. As an inclusive community it is important to teach children about respect for cultural differences and to celebrate diversity. Trainees who grab the moment are able to value children's home experiences and use these as a context for learning in the classroom. This is empowering for children and provides them with a sense of belonging.

Children may come to school and ask questions. They may have seen a rainbow for the first time during the journey to school and they may ask the teacher questions about it. They may want to know what it is and how it has formed. Confident teachers are able to capitalise on children's immediate interests and use them as a basis for developing sustained shared thinking. The REPEY research defines sustained shared thinking as:

> ... an episode in which two or more individuals 'work together' in an intellectual way to solve a problem, clarify a concept, evaluate activities, extend a narrative ... both parties must contribute to the thinking and it must develop and extend. (Siraj-Blatchford et al., 2002: 8)

The research found that in effective settings dialogues between children and adults were characterised by sustained shared thinking and that staff with higher qualifications encouraged more sustained shared thinking than staff with lower qualifications. This research has implications for the way in which adult–child interactions are conducted. In your interactions with children you should seek to extend children's thinking through good quality questioning and through working with children to extend their thought processes. Children's questions could be a good starting point for developing sustained shared thinking but rather than giving them answers you could extend their understanding through further questioning, modelling and researching with the child so that they discover the new learning for themselves. In this way excellent practitioners develop the skill of scaffolding children's learning (see Bruner, 1996).

📁 **Case study**

Lilijana was teaching a class of children aged 4–5 years. A small group of children were playing in the water tray with sponge balls. Lilijana was supporting them. The transcript of the conversation between a child and Lilijana is shown below:

Child: Look the ball is going under the water now! Why did it do that?
Teacher: Yes it was floating and now it is beginning to sink. That's a good question.

(Continued)

(Continued)

Child: How did that happen?
Teacher: I am not sure, what do you think? How shall we find the answer?
Child: It's because it is heavy.
Teacher: So why did it float in the beginning?
Child: It wasn't heavy then?
Teacher: What made it become heavy?
Child: It has got water in it now.
Teacher: So how can you make it float again?
           [*Child grabs the ball and squeezes the water out of it and places the ball back on the surface of the water.*]
Teacher: What is the ball doing now?
Child: It is floating.
Teacher: What is it going to do?
Child: It will get filled with water and sink.
Teacher: You're right!
           [*Lilijana then collects a rubber ball and places it on the surface of the water and they both watch it.*]
Child: It is still floating.
Teacher: Why isn't it sinking like the sponge ball?
Child: Because the water can't get in.

Reflection

> How did the teacher scaffold the child's language?
> How did the teacher capitalise on the child's play to promote learning?
> How did the teacher demonstrate respect for the child's ideas and develop these further?
> Carefully analyse the types of questions the teacher used to support learning.

Young children are curious and often ask many questions. Avoid the temptation to brush these questions aside if you do not know the answers. Demonstrate to your learners that you are also a learner and enjoy the challenge of finding out the answers to the children's questions together. This process enables you to model the skill of how to be a learner and this is fundamentally more important than having all the answers to children's questions at your fingertips. Children's interests and questions can then be used as a context for developing learning across the curriculum for the rest of the day or week. It takes confidence to demonstrate this level of flexibility but by the end of your training you should become less reliant on minute-by-minute session plans.

Trainees who grab the moment are able to respond to events that take place during the school day. The children's interests may be ignited through a stimulating act of collective workship or by an event that they have experienced before they arrived at school. Demonstrating flexibility in your teaching will require you to tune into your learners. You will need to listen to them, talk with them and observe them to find out what they are interested in at that specific time. Providing your learners with opportunities to lead the learning in this way for some of the time is a powerful way of raising their self-esteem.

However, we wish to emphasise that it is not appropriate to abandon planning all of the time or to do little or no planning in the name of flexibility. You need to remember that planning and the identification of clear learning objectives and learning outcomes are key professional requirements that need to be demonstrated to achieve the QTS standards. Additionally, planning for progression is also a requirement of the standards. Therefore we are not advocating a completely child-centred approach. We do, however, feel that children (and teachers) can benefit from a degree of flexibility some of the time and that this flexibility might allow you to respond to children's questions, interests or unplanned sudden events.

Within early years and primary education it is often unhelpful to confine learning to specific time slots. Children may need longer than thirty minutes to write a powerful story or they may resist being told to tidy away when they are making a new product in design and technology. If children are absorbed in a particular piece of learning it is educationally sound to allow them to continue into the next session rather than asking them to stop. It is difficult to pick something up again a week later. Grabbing the moment, by allowing children to immerse themselves in deep learning, demonstrates flexibility in your approach. However, you will need to think through carefully how you organise this and you will need to discuss it with your class mentor. It may be possible to combine some structured sessions with sessions that allow children opportunities to carry learning over from one session to the next.

Inspiring learners

Outstanding trainees inspire and motivate learners through teaching creative, innovative lessons which make a lasting impression on their memories. One trainee asked the children to be scientists in one lesson I observed. She told them that a company employed them and that their job was to investigate which type of paper out of a selection was the best for mopping up spills. She gave each child a white laboratory coat to wear and they spent the entire lesson carrying out important scientific investigation work for the company. Creating such a context increases learner motivation and fosters pupil participation. It provides children with a purpose for their learning and adds a new dimension. Further guidance on creative teaching is included in Chapter 4. These lessons are interesting and relevant and foster frequent opportunities for pupil participation.

Demonstrating a passion for learning

Outstanding trainees demonstrate a love of learning and they communicate this to their learners consistently. This passion for learning emerges in their teaching. During periods of school-based placement you need to be energetic in the classroom. You need to communicate enthusiasm through verbal and non-verbal forms of communication. You need to show your learners (and mentors and tutors) that you are genuinely excited about what you are teaching and you can do this through varying your voice tone and facial expressions. You need to demonstrate to your learners that you enjoy learning from them. They need to see you as a learner as well as a teacher and outstanding trainees model being a learner very effectively. In some lessons you may be able to create opportunities to sit alongside children to enable you to model being a learner. Outstanding trainees can switch from teacher mode to learner mode within a lesson. In the EYFS you might model being a leaner by playing alongside children or by reading a book to yourself in the reading area. You might work alongside children in the writing area so that you can model being a writer. Throughout the primary years you might work alongside children in art and design and technology by creating your own products. There are many ways that you can communicate a passion for learning. You need to create the spaces and opportunities to model the learning process.

Thinking creatively and being innovative

Outstanding trainees are lateral thinkers. They demonstrate the ability to plan and teach lessons which are original, creative and engaging. These lessons are planned with clear learning objectives and learning outcomes in mind. However, these are taught creatively. These lessons make an impact on learners because they remember them several months or even years later.

Cremin (2009) argues that creative teachers frequently provide children with time and space to experiment. She argues that they develop a pedagogy which is based on trust and respect for children's ideas. A creative pedagogy provides children with the freedom to organise their own learning and make their own decisions (Cremin, 2009). Creative teachers are open to new ideas and encourage children to see the relevance and purpose of tasks they are asked to undertake (Cremin, 2009).

There is a growing market in which trainees and teachers can obtain commercially produced lesson plans. The internet now enables trainees to download lesson plans and schemes of work, often free of charge. Companies have been established that provide lesson plans which cover the entire curriculum from the EYFS to Year 6 and beyond. These 'off the shelf' lessons may be useful for stimulating your thinking and giving you ideas. However, they will rarely meet the specific needs of *your* learners. You are unlikely to deliver creative, inspirational, innovative lessons if you rely on commercially produced material. Trainees who achieve outstanding outcomes demonstrate the ability to think for themselves. They are able to provide learners with rich contexts and clear purposes of learning. They demonstrate an ability to plan meaningful links between areas of the curriculum and their lessons excite, motivate and energise *their* learners. No class has the same needs and this is where commercially produced material falls short.

Outstanding trainees may teach lessons in ways that are original and using approaches that have not been tried before. These lessons will foster high levels of learner participation and children will make rapid progress because they are engaged. The best trainees are not 'technicians' who merely deliver lessons they have read in a book or downloaded from the internet. They are *educators* who demonstrate the ability to think creatively and imaginatively and consequently bring learning to life. These trainees do their best to ensure that every lesson makes an impact and leaves a lasting impression on their learners. Ofsted inspectors, tutors and mentors long to see lessons that they have never seen before. Worksheets are unlikely to impress and often result in dull, uninspiring teaching. The aim of teaching is to foster the development of pupils' thinking and filling in boxes on worksheets tends to stifle this. Try to think of an alternative way of teaching a concept rather than using a worksheet. Make the learning vivid, practical and fun. Remember that the outcomes of every lesson do not always have to result in recorded work. You can record the learning in many other ways with a little imagination. Examples of alternative ways of recording learning and evidencing achievement are through the use of photographs, written observations, digital and audio recording.

Being reflective

Outstanding trainees are able to reflect critically and rigorously on their own practice and take action to continually improve their practice. To demonstrate this you will need to show that you have a depth of insight into the strengths and weaknesses of your own practice. Your ability to critically reflect will be evidenced through:

> detailed lesson and weekly evaluations;
> discussions with your mentor about your teaching – these should be daily, weekly and at the mid and end points of your placement.

Try not to be descriptive in your evaluations. Demonstrate to your mentors that you know what aspects of your practice need to be improved and identify the actions that you need to take to achieve your targets. Outstanding trainees often involve teachers and teaching assistants in the evaluation of their practice; they value their advice and take action on the basis of it.

In post-lesson feedback and meetings where progress is reviewed, outstanding trainees are able to articulate clearly their own strengths and areas for development. In these meetings outstanding trainees take an active role and they are able to make well-founded judgements about their own performance. These trainees do not rely on mentors or link tutors to make assessments of their teaching because they are able to rate their own performance and justify their judgements. These trainees are able to demonstrate a clear audit trail throughout their placement. This trail should identify:

> key targets for the placement (through an action plan);
> regular reflections on progress towards these initial targets;
> regular identification of targets on a weekly basis;
> evidence of implementation of strategies to address these weekly targets;
> evidence of further evaluation following implementation of strategies.

Pollard argues that 'maintaining a constructive engagement, a willingness to imagine new futures and a self-critical spirit are thus all connected to reflective practice' (2005: 19). He emphasises that the ability to posses an open mind is essential for rigorous reflection.

Taking control of your own professional development

Outstanding trainees are able to take control of their own professional development. They are able to identify targets for their own development and take appropriate action to address these. During your placement you should take regular opportunities to meet with relevant professionals who will be able to help you address your targets. If you have a specific weakness with assessment then it would be useful for you to arrange a meeting with the assessment leader. It might be possible to work jointly on assessing children's learning/work or carry out some joint moderation. If you struggle with planning for specific aspects of literacy, arrange a tutorial with the literacy subject leader. If you are allocated professional development time, use this time productively to work on your specific targets. Outstanding trainees are able to identify key targets and actions to be taken themselves rather than being directed by their mentors. Prior to undertaking a block placement meet with your academic tutor to reflect on your previous placement and draw up an action plan to address your targets. Discuss ways in which you might address these targets with your tutor.

Being respected

Outstanding trainees are highly respected by colleagues, learners and parents/carers. In order to gain respect you have to show that you respect others. You might consider the following:

> show others that you are interested in what they have to say by listening to them and making good eye contact;
> value other people's ideas and support other colleagues in school;
> minimise power differentials by creating a team ethos; ensure that the contributions of all team members are valued;
> show children that you like them and are interested in them as people – value them as individuals and not just as learners;
> be honest with people;
> demonstrate to colleagues, parents and carers that you are a truly dedicated professional and are worthy of joining the teaching profession;
> ensure that parents and carers know that you value their child;
> involve yourself in the life of the school as you are part of a whole school team;
> be organised and plan thoroughly;
> ensure that punctuality and attendance are exemplary.

Reflection

Reflect on the above list and think carefully about ways in which you might address each point.

Staff in school will expect you to work hard and show commitment and resilience. Teaching is an increasingly demanding profession and you will get tired. You should expect this towards the second half of your placement but you should continue working to maximum capacity. You are accountable on many different levels and you will gain little respect if you continually complain about feeling tired.

Demonstrating the capacity to be an outstanding teacher

Outstanding trainees are not outstanding teachers. Outstanding trainees demonstrate the *capacity* to be outstanding teachers. They teach lessons that are often good and often show *characteristics* of outstanding lessons. To achieve the best outcomes on your teaching placement you therefore need to demonstrate that you have the capacity to be an outstanding teacher in the future. To demonstrate this capacity you should:

> consistently act on advice and demonstrate improvements;
> demonstrate insight into wider issues associated with teaching and learning and suggest ways of developing strategies for enhancing parent partnership or improving the standard of children's writing;
> demonstrate the ability to consistently critically reflect on your own practice and make necessary changes;
> begin to use assessment data to set pupils challenging targets which raise standards;
> begin to use assessment data to identify group and individual needs;
> experiment with creative, original, innovative teaching strategies;
> create a highly effective stimulating learning environment which is conducive to learning.

Demonstrating the capacity for leadership

Your ITT provider will not expect you to lead staff meetings during periods of school-based training. You are, after all, there to learn! You also do not want to appear to be arrogant. However, there are subtle ways in which you can demonstrate your capacity for leadership.

The easiest and most obvious way to demonstrate this is to start with the team in your classroom. It is likely that there will be other adults working along-side you in the classroom whose role it is to support you. Ensure that you communicate with these adults frequently about their roles and responsibili-ties and develop your confidence by delegating tasks to them. Ensure that all adults working with you are clear about what you expect and that they know the learning outcomes of the activities for the groups of learners they are working with. Involve these adults in the planning process, ask for their ideas and empower them by giving them responsibility. Involve them in the assess-ment process by asking them to make simple records about the children they are working with. A simple briefing sheet, with space for them to write comments about children's progress, is an effective way of ensuring that communication is a two-way process.

Some trainees find it difficult to delegate tasks to more experienced professionals. You need to think carefully about your tone of voice and body language when you communicate with others. Additionally you need to value the ideas and opinions of colleagues and acknowledge their contributions. Do not be afraid to seek support and advice from members of the team, including support staff.

Ask to be involved in team meetings, especially planning meetings, and take an active role in these by making contributions. If you have visited other schools to observe practice then take the opportunity to share this with staff at meet-ings. Remember that schools are a learning community and effective teachers are usually receptive to new ideas. Play a full role and ensure that you contribute to the life of the school by involving yourself in extra-curricular activities. Share research and practice which you have been introduced to with your school-based colleagues. Many of them will welcome this opportunity to develop their own learning. Much of this can be done informally and ad hoc during the place-ment. Show your mentors that you are keen to share your knowledge but that you are also eager to learn from them.

Professional development

Ask your ITT provider to give you details of teachers who embed creative approaches into their practice. Your provider may have contacts with ASTs who are experts in creative practice. Make arrangements to visit one of these profes-sionals in school and observe them teaching. Make a note of strategies which they use to engage their learners. Follow the observations with a tutorial with the teacher. Discuss ideas for embedding creativity across the curriculum.

Link to research

Research into creative teaching is extensive. Observations of creative class-room practice can be found in key literature (Jeffrey and Woods, 2003; Cremin, Burnard and Craft, 2006). There is also a large volume of work on the character traits of creative teachers which you will find useful (Fryer, 1996; Beetlestone, 1998). Jeffrey and Woods have written extensively about creative teaching, inno-vation and ownership of the curriculum (Woods and Jeffrey, 1996; Jeffrey and Woods, 2003; Jeffrey, 2006).

Further reading

Medwell, J. (2007) *Successful Teaching Placement: Primary and Early Years.* Exeter: Learning Matters.
This text provides a very comprehensive overview of the things you need to think about before, during and after a teaching placement. There is useful advice on planning, teaching and assessment, and general advice about coping with the challenges of placement. This text should be a core text on your reading list.

Useful websites

www.ltscotland.org.uk/creativity/index.asp
This website provides a useful selection of documents on creativity in education and several case studies of good practice from a range of educational settings.

www.teachers.tv/
The Teacher's TV website contains a wealth of video clips of good lessons. There are specific video clips on creative approaches and useful interviews with teachers.

2

Professional knowledge and understanding

This chapter covers

This chapter addresses the wider policy context which affects teaching and offers practical suggestions for embedding the key messages from current educational policy into your practice. We emphasise the importance of meeting the specific individual needs of learners and providing effective personalised provision to meet their needs. We also address the importance of teaching children to value and respect diversity and the necessity to challenge prejudice and discrimination.

According to Ofsted outstanding trainees:

> describe the stages in progress through a topic/set of ideas and concepts/sequence of teaching – explaining what they would look for in learners;

> can give examples of lessons, and individual/groups of learners, to illustrate this – including the identification of barriers to learning and how these were/can be overcome;

> are able to discuss in detail individual learners' progress as well as attainment/achievement;

> are able to use their depth of subject-specific pedagogical understanding to explain in detail why they use particular teaching approaches and why these are likely to be more successful than others;

> demonstrate an understanding of the range of professionals that contribute to learners' overall development and their place in the 'bigger picture' – well-informed discussion about individual/groups of learners and particular needs;
> show a depth of understanding of the implications of Every Child Matters across a wide range of work and how to promote learners' understanding and exploit the potential provided by social and cultural diversity. (2009: 34)

In this chapter we examine these criteria and suggest ways in which you may demonstrate them during your teaching placement. This chapter focuses on barriers to learning for specific groups the implications of the wider educational policy agenda which schools are required to address and multi-agency collaboration. In addition the chapter examine your understanding of progression in learning and the importance of subject knowledge.

Barriers to learning

The National Curriculum (DfEE, 1999) identifies three important principles to develop inclusive approaches. Schools and teachers should:

> set suitable learning challenges;
> respond to pupils' diverse learning needs;
> overcome potential barriers to learning and assessment for individuals and groups of pupils. (1999: 30)

These principles form the basis of the current educational agenda and this will be discussed later in the chapter. The full breadth and balance of the National Curriculum is a statutory entitlement for every child. Consequently this places a statutory duty on schools to provide all children with opportunities to access the knowledge, skills and understanding outlined in the National Curriculum (Knowles, 2006). This ensures that all children are provided with equality of opportunity throughout their education. The Disability Discrimination Act (2005) places a statutory duty on schools to make 'reasonable adjustments' to provision to ensure that all learners are provided with equality of opportunity.

During your teaching placements you may encounter children with specific barriers to learning and participation. These may be:

> learners with special educational needs and disabilities;
> travellers, refugees and asylum seekers;
> children from diverse social and cultural backgrounds;

> children from diverse linguistic backgrounds;
> children who are identified as gifted or talented;
> children with behavioural, emotional and social difficulties.

This is not an exhaustive list and this chapter cannot do justice to each of these categories. Instead this chapter provides general advice in relation to the types of strategies and approaches that might be relevant. It is crucial to remember that all learners are individuals. Children with ASD do not constitute one homogenous group. Generic strategies might not work with every child. You should aim to develop strategies to remove barriers to learning in consultation with your mentor(s), parents, carers and the child. Equally, it is important not to categorise learners with specific needs by wrongly assuming that they have special educational needs.

It is likely that you will encounter children with specific needs. The needs of individual learners should be discussed fully with your class mentor. You are likely to be required to undertake pre-placement visits and you should take the opportunity to identify such needs. Additionally there may be an opportunity for you to discuss specific needs with a university or training provider tutor who is a specialist is in this field. Your class mentor will hopefully provide you with some suggestions on how barriers to learning and participation can be addressed. However, outstanding trainees will undertake personal research into the specific needs of the children in their class. This research could include the following:

> reading articles, books and chapters about a specific need;
> researching information on the internet;
> researching case studies of 'interventions' from practising teachers (teacher-researchers) who have adopted an action research methodology;
> speaking to external colleagues who may be involved in supporting the child.

Outstanding trainees are willing to try out new interventions and evaluate the success of these. There is an expectation in the *Special Educational Needs Code of Practice* (DfES, 2001) that parents and carers should be consulted and their views and advice should be sought. There is also an expectation that parents and carers should be involved in setting and reviewing targets. This open communication with parents will lead to productive relationships and you should develop systems for facilitating communication between home and school. The Code of Practice also emphasises the importance of consulting children, involving children in setting and reviewing targets, and actively seeking their views about their education. These are sound principles to adopt when working with any child with specific needs.

Specific barriers to learning can be identified through carefully observing children over a period of time. For children with specific learning needs we recommend that you spend some of your early placement visits observing the child and talking to practitioners and parents/carers about their needs. This will be time well spent.

Outstanding trainees are able to develop highly effective relationships with all learners. You therefore need to spend some time establishing these. It may take you longer to establish positive relationships with some children but you should work at this by spending time with them and showing a personal interest in them.

To remove specific barriers to learning, the approaches that you adopt will largely depend on the specific needs of the child. Some children will need access to additional resources or specialist equipment to aid their learning. Children with social, emotional and behavioural issues might benefit from a less rigid timetable with short blocks of 'chunked' learning. Children with communication and interaction difficulties may benefit from the use of visual timetables, visual instructions or picture-exchange communication systems. All of these strategies could be termed 'reasonable adjustments' to the standard provision. The key point to bear in mind is that inclusion necessitates additional and different provision for equality of opportunity rather than all learners accessing the same provision. You will need to ensure that learning tasks are appropriately differentiated to meet the needs of individuals and groups.

Case study

Frances was placed in a large urban school for her final teaching placement. On her first day in the school Frances discovered that she would be teaching a boy called Oliver who had a diagnosis of ASD. Oliver had limited language and found social interaction with his peers very difficult. Additionally he quickly became distressed when he was asked to do something new.

Frances had no prior experience of working with children with ASD. After talking to the class mentor about his specific needs, Frances decided to undertake some personal research. She visited the library and discovered a wealth of literature relating to the condition. Frances also researched information on the internet about ASD. During one of her placement visits a specialist support worker came into school to support Oliver. Frances seized the opportunity to observe the session and she noted down some of the strategies that were being used with Oliver during the session. At the end of the session Frances spoke to the support worker about Oliver's specific needs and strategies for addressing these.

During the observations prior to her placement, Frances had noted that Oliver had difficulty with understanding even short verbal instructions. Frances had read about a strategy called 'story strip'. This strategy uses visual images to depict how to complete a given task. Frances initially trialled the use of the strategy during a PE lesson. The strategy was successful. Oliver was able to collect his PE bag and get changed. Using the visual prompts Oliver was able to remove only the necessary items of clothing. During his time in the gym he was able to complete a short sequence of given tasks in order. At the end of the lesson Oliver was able to put his clothing back on in order.

Following this Frances discussed the use of the strategy across the curriculum with her class mentor and Oliver's parents. She trialled the strategy in lessons where Oliver was required to complete specific tasks. Frances set up a home–school diary to record Oliver's responses to the strategy and his responses to specific tasks.

Reflection

> How might the approaches adopted by Frances be used to support other learners with specific needs?

Current policy agenda

The current educational policy agenda aims to improve educational outcomes for all children. The agenda places a particular focus on early intervention for vulnerable and disadvantaged children which include:

> children with learning difficulties and disabilities;
> children in public care;
> travellers, refugees and asylum seekers;
> children living in families where parents have alcohol or drug dependency problems or a mental illness;
> children affected by domestic violence.

Clearly a range of external factors affect children's learning and development. The professional standards for QTS require you to demonstrate that you are aware of the influences which affect achievement. Children's self-esteem and self-concept can be affected by the issues they experience in their lives outside school. If children do not feel loved or safe, then it will be difficult for them to learn effectively at school. Children's sense of personal well-being affects their performance in school. Teachers are accountable and must demonstrate that they have provided effective personalised provision to meet the needs of specific children. They have a responsibility to ensure that every child fulfils their education potential, regardless of each child's personal circumstances.

Initially you should discuss any vulnerable children with your class mentor. All information relating to specific children must remain confidential and you may not be allowed to keep written notes about individual children. Discuss with your class mentor strategies for supporting vulnerable children and the types of interventions which are feasible for you to trial on your teaching placement. Find out if specific children are supported by other school-based colleagues or external agencies and create opportunities to meet with relevant personnel to discuss the needs of specific children. During your placement plan activities and interventions in collaboration with support staff and, where possible, actively seek opportunities to facilitate open communication with parents and carers. Schools will already have in place strategies for learners with special educational needs and you will be required to adopt these to ensure that there is consistency of practice with the child.

Outstanding trainees are able to plan innovative approaches to address children's individual needs. You should identify on your lesson plans how the needs of individuals or groups of children will be met.

The following approaches could be used to address the holistic needs of all learners and prepare them for their future lives:

> teaching children about healthy eating and the benefits of physical activity;
> teaching children about bullying and addressing issues related to bullying if they arise;
> developing enterprise projects to develop pupils' understanding of team work, money, profit and loss, planning and marketing;
> developing a range of approaches through which children can express their views;
> planning activities to enable children to make a positive contribution to their school or local community;
> developing peer-mentoring schemes or 'befriending' schemes, for example playtime buddies or peer subject mentors;
> developing peer mediation as a strategy to reduce incidents of bullying;
> developing relaxation techniques, for example peer massage (a website link for peer massage is provided at the end of this chapter). (Adapted from Cheminais, 2006)

Many of the approaches identified above will be part of whole-school policies and it is important that you familiarise yourself with these before you start your placement. However, outstanding trainees will also research into alternative approaches for addressing the broad educational policy context within their placement. An example is illustrated through the following case study.

Case study

Ben was keen to develop his pupils' understanding of sustainability. He was undertaking his final placement in a primary school situated within an area of social deprivation. He was responsible for a Year 6 class. Ben decided to research further into the sustainable schools agenda on the internet. He found out about the various strands of sustainability (known as the eight doorways) from the TeacherNet site. Ben decided to focus on the strand relating to 'global dimension' as it fitted in well with the class theme 'India'.

He made links with a national charity which worked with Ben to develop an enterprise project. The aim was to raise money so that the charity could fund a water supply for the village. Ben asked the children to identify the product that they wished to make and sell to raise money for the charity. The children voted to form a toy company which was responsible for making and selling toys. This work provided a good vehicle for the development of children's design and technology skills. Children were divided into teams and took turns in planning and designing, making, selling and marketing products.

In geography children researched into the geography of the area and they sent letters to children in a school in the village. At the end of the placement the children raised £300 which was then forwarded to the charity to go towards purchasing a water pump for the rural community in India.

Reflection

> What links could be made to develop learning across the curriculum with this type of project?
> What purposeful opportunities could this project create for developing the pupils' writing and speaking and listening skills?

Social and cultural diversity
The community cohesion agenda seeks to promote the development of community cohesion through:

> enabling children to respect cultural differences;
> encouraging children from different cultural backgrounds to interact with each other;

> positively celebrating diversity and embracing diversity through teaching resources and activities;
> challenging racist and discriminatory attitudes.

Your school will be taking steps to address community cohesion as school inspections focus closely on this aspect. You should therefore find out about the school policy in relation to community cohesion and ensure that you are taking steps to address the points within it.

Challenging prejudice and discrimination

Children may, advertently or inadvertently, develop negative stereotypes in relation to groups of individuals. Often these stereotypes relate to minority groups. Negative perceptions can be formed in the home, the wider community or with peers and should always be challenged. Young children do not always understand what they are saying and such issues must be dealt with in a sensitive manner. It is necessary to establish the level of understanding held by the child in relation to their comments or actions towards others. Be aware that the values of the school may contradict the values instilled at home. Professionals have a moral duty to promote positive attitudes towards all groups and should always address issues related to prejudice and discrimination. The following process may help you to deal with such incidents.

> Ask the child what they have said or done.
> Then ask them if they understand what their words or actions mean.
> Calmly explain that such words or actions are hurtful, unfair and inappropriate under any circumstances.
> Ask the child how they would feel if they were targeted with similar words or actions.
> Ask the child how they wish to resolve the issue.

Case study

Emily and Nick were both planning to develop children's understanding of community cohesion on their final teaching placement. Nick was placed in a multicultural school with a predominantly Asian population. Emily was placed in a rural school serving a middle-class white British community. Both trainees were teaching in KS2.

Emily and Nick decided to carry out a video conferencing project between the two schools. Essentially this enabled the children from both schools to talk to each other over a live video link. Both trainees discussed the project before hand with the nominated e-safety representative and aspects relating to e-safety were discussed with the children prior to 'going live'.

The video conferencing project enabled children from both schools to find out about different aspects relating to their culture. A different focus was selected each week and included food, festivals and celebrations, religious beliefs and leisure. Prior to each session, the children were provided with opportunities to think about questions they wanted to ask. These were written down and presented to each class before the session so that both classes had time to prepare their responses. In addition to the video conferencing sessions children from each school had the opportunity to undertake a planned visit to the other school.

Reflection

> What issues would be presented in terms of e-safety?
> What issues would be presented in relation to parental values and how might these be overcome?
> How can this project link to other aspects of the curriculum, such as writing, religious education, geography or citizenship education?

Multi-agency working and parent partnership

The current educational policy agenda emphasises the importance of teachers working in partnership with other agencies to raise outcomes for learners. In addition the agenda focuses on developing effective partnerships with parent and carers in order to raise levels of attainment. You will need to find out whether specific children's learning needs are supported by other professionals outside school. These might include:

> educational psychologists;
> behaviour support workers;
> speech and language therapists;
> physiotherapists;
> specialist support teachers, for example hearing or visual impaired teacher or teacher of autistic learners.

There may be challenges associated with developing parent partnerships. Some parents may be reluctant to engage with education for a variety of reasons. What might these be? You will not successfully develop effective partnerships with all parents but you need to create opportunities through which parents and carers can communicate with you and work in partnership with you to raise levels of attainment. A useful starting point in developing effective partnerships with parents is to be approachable, listen to their concerns, take them seriously and act upon them. Outstanding trainees will develop effective communication with parents through the use of daily diaries, information leaflets to inform them about their child's targets and ways in which they may support their child with these, and class newsletters to inform parents and carers about curriculum coverage. Before developing initiatives you should discuss these with your mentor(s) and ensure that you are working within school policies. Opportunities may present themselves for you to involve parents and carers in the classroom. You could develop specific initiatives to engage fathers in supporting learning in the classroom. You can make good use of the school's virtual learning environment to develop effective communication with parents. There is a wealth of possibilities and you should capitalise on some of these during your placement.

 Professional development

Research into case studies of practice related to parent partnership. Research into initiatives for:

> developing effective communication with parents and carers;
> developing approaches to enable parents to work with their own children to raise their levels of attainment;
> developing parental involvement in the classroom;
> developing parental knowledge of aspects of the taught curriculum.

Identify specific strategies that you might be able to implement during your teaching placement. Discuss these with your mentor.

Progress and attainment

Outstanding trainees have an intuitive knowledge of the learners they teach. They are able to discuss in detail individual learners' progress, achievement and attainment in specific subjects and strands of subjects. They have an intuitive knowledge of the stages children have reached in their learning and their next steps. Outstanding trainees are able to articulate this information to colleagues and use the information to plan for subsequent learning. Their knowledge is supported by robust assessments but outstanding trainees do not constantly need to refer to assessment documentation to help them talk about their learners.

To develop this intuitive knowledge of your learners you need to spend time observing them and working closely with them as individuals and during small group work. You should spend your initial visits to your placement school getting to know your learners. Spend time talking to the practitioners who you will be working alongside to develop your knowledge of the children. During your placement enhance your knowledge of the children by talking to parents and carers about their child's learning. This will be easier if the school operates an open-door policy. Continue frequent dialogue with the colleagues working alongside you about the learners you are supporting. Develop dialogue with children through regular 'learning conversations' about their progress, achievement and attainment. Children have a unique knowledge of their own strengths and learning needs and seeking children's perspectives about their learning will provide you with rich information to enhance the assessment process.

Subject knowledge

Outstanding trainees are able to identify and use effective teaching approaches to enable children to access the learning. This pedagogical subject knowledge is just as important as knowledge of the concepts, skills and understanding associated with specific subjects. Confident trainees are able to use a wide range of teaching strategies to support their teaching. It is important to plan to use a combination of visual, auditory and kinaesthetic strategies to cater for a range of learning styles. A lesson which over-uses auditory strategies (for example oral explanations) is unlikely to be effective. Learning can be maximised if explanations are also supported by visual approaches and if children have the opportunity to learn through first-hand experiences. The three strategies can work effectively in combination. These strategies can be supported by effective questioning and careful teacher modelling. This application of learning style theory into practice can help all learners to access the curriculum. Some learners may have a preferential learning style. It is possible that some learners may prefer to learn through the use of visual strategies, for example. However, effective learners are able to learn through all three approaches. Rather than categorising learners as having a specific learning style, it is more productive to plan lessons which make use of all three approaches.

Teacher modelling

Teacher modelling is a useful strategy for developing children's knowledge, skills, attitudes and understanding. Through modelling the teacher transmits intended expectations to learners. These may include:

> expectations of behaviour;
> the use of language, for example using technical vocabulary related to learning;
> the use of mutual respect;
> appropriate ways of listening to others and valuing the contributions of others;
> transmitting the expectation that others will listen to you;
> communicating needs in appropriate ways through appropriate interactions;
> appropriate responses to experiences;
> turn taking;
> modelling the processes of reading, writing, speaking and listening;
> modelling how to solve mathematical problems;
> modelling how to craft a piece of writing;
> modelling specific skills and techniques, for example how to use a pencil or paintbrush.

Professional development

Imagine that you are teaching a KS1 class about the concept of multiplication as repeated addition. You start off by explaining this idea. Working with a colleague, discuss how you could apply learning style theory to enable all learners to access the learning.

Link to research

The EPPE research (Sylva et al., 2004) found that when pre-school settings encouraged high levels of parent engagement in children's learning, this resulted in intellectual gains for the children. This research identified that children made better cognitive gains where educational aims were shared with parents. This enabled parents to support learning at home and complement the learning which was taking place in the setting. Additionally the research found that social class and parental qualifications were less significant than what parents did in terms of parental engagement.

Further reading

Knowles, G. (ed.) (2006) *Supporting Inclusive Practice*. London: David Fulton.
This text provides a very comprehensive overview of different categories of special educational needs and offers guidance relating to strategies for breaking down barriers to learning.

Useful websites

www.teachernet.gov.uk/sustainableschools/index.cfm
This site provides useful information about the sustainable schools agenda.

www.education.gov.uk/schools/careers/traininganddevelopment/research-informedpractice
This link provides access to practitioner research in education.

www.schoolslinkingnetwork.org.uk/
This site provides valuable information on developing pupils' understanding of cultural diversity and the community cohesion agenda. There are case studies representing good practice and there is some access to resources.

www.jrf.org.uk/
This site provides academic articles on the impact of factors such as social class, ethnicity and social deprivation on pupil attainment. This is very useful in terms of supporting trainees with academic assignments.

www.massageinschoolsassociation.org.uk/index.php?massageinschools
This site provides a brief overview of the technique of peer massage.

3

Planning for teaching
and learning

This chapter covers

Throughout this chapter we introduce the key principles of effective planning. We stress that your planning should be sufficiently flexible to cater for children's emerging learning needs. In addition we argue that effective planning is dependent on accurate prior assessments of children's knowledge, skills and understanding. Your planning should help to evidence many professional standards for QTS. Without accurate assessment of children's learning you will find it difficult to differentiate your teaching to meet children's needs. Additionally you will find it difficult to demonstrate high expectations of your learners without accurate differentiation. Your planning will help to evidence your understanding of progression in children's learning, thus demonstrating accurate pedagogical subject knowledge. Your plans will outline the range of teaching approaches used to support learning, and links to assessment opportunities will be evident. You will also be able to evidence your ability to use the statutory and non-statutory curriculum frameworks through your planning. Your planning (and evaluations) helps your mentors and tutors to build up a complete picture of your personal learning journey through your placement. Outstanding trainees recognise the importance of effective, detailed and precise planning as a pre-requisite to effective teaching.

Why do you need to plan?

Trainee teachers are often overwhelmed with the amount of planning they are required to do during their teaching placements. Planning takes time and effort and is hard work. Additionally trainees often work alongside experienced teachers who may do less planning than they are expected to do. So why do you need to plan in such detail? The first point to stress is that you are not an experienced teacher. You do not have the benefit of several years of experience to draw upon. Consequently you need to think through your lessons in far more detail than your colleagues may have to do in school. When producing your plans you will need to give due consideration to the following:

> progression within a strand of learning: developing children's knowledge, skills and understanding over a period of time;
> what you want the children to learn in your lessons;
> how children will demonstrate success;
> how you will structure learning within a lesson and between lessons;
> the resources that you will need;
> the key questions you need to ask in your lessons;
> how you will cater for children's diverse learning needs within a lesson;
> what you want to assess.

As a trainee teacher you do not have the experience to do all of the above in your head. Effective and detailed planning is no guarantee that your lessons will be effective or even go according to plan. However, if your lessons are not planned effectively they will almost certainly not be outstanding. Effective and detailed planning increases the chances of your lessons running smoothly.

The internet now includes a wealth of information to support teachers' planning. Additionally commercial companies have been established to provide teachers with resources and lesson plans. Although this will save you a great deal of time it is important to remember that no purchased (or downloaded) plan can ever fully meet the specific needs of the diverse range of learners in your class. Effective primary teachers adapt their planning on a day-to-day basis to meet the emerging learning needs of the children in their class. Planning should therefore be seen as flexible and fluid rather than static. If a group of learners has struggled with a concept in a specific lesson, this concept will need to be revisited and revised in the next lesson before you can move onto a new concept. In this way your ongoing formative assessments should drive your planning. Commercial schemes and lesson plans are useful for providing you with ideas but must not be followed slavishly. You therefore need to bring to your planning your own knowledge of what your learners need.

School and training provider policies

Your ITT provider will have introduced you to the principles of effective planning and you may have been provided with specific planning formats to support you in the process of planning for children's learning. However, these are usually issued as guidance only. You should adapt planning frameworks so that they meet your needs.

Your school may have specific planning formats in place. You need to establish whether your school expect you to use the school planning formats or whether there is some flexibility. Before adopting the school formats it is important to check that these include all the information required by your ITT provider. Sometimes it is possible to slightly adapt the school planning frameworks by including the additional aspects required by your ITT provider. This often keeps all parties happy!

Levels of planning

Medium-term planning
The medium-term plans are the outlines of your teaching. They are often referred to as schemes of work. A medium-term plan should show the intended coverage of objectives within a specific subject throughout the duration of the block placement. Medium-term planning may be specific to one subject or be cross curricular. This will depend on the approach to planning adopted by the school. You will be expected to complete all your medium-term plans before you start any teaching for all subjects where you will be teaching a sequence of lessons. In writing medium-term plans you will need to bring together your ideas, the school's long-term planning, the resources you will need and consideration of how you are going to teach and assess the work. Your medium-term plans must be sufficiently detailed for you to be able to draw upon them to produce useful weekly and daily lesson plans but should avoid the fine detail, which belongs in the lesson/session plan. Please note that if schools adopt commercial schemes of work to support the development of medium-term plans, you are expected to adapt these. You should modify the school's medium-term plans and demonstrate innovation within a scheme of work. This is a key opportunity to demonstrate creativity and lateral thinking.

Weekly planning
In KS1, and sometimes in the EYFS, weekly planners should be completed for each week for mathematics and literacy. You will need to review this planning

as a result of evaluating your teaching and the children's achievements, and modifications will need to be made on a daily basis to weekly plans. The purpose of the weekly plan is to show the intended coverage of objectives over the course of the week and ways in which learning will progress for specific groups of learners.

Weekly plans are developed from medium-term plans and lesson plans are developed from weekly plans. The various levels of planning should be evident in your planning and teaching file.

Lesson plans

The purpose of a lesson plan is to identify:

> what children will learn in a lesson (objectives);
> what the role of the teacher and additional adults will be;
> what the children will be doing;
> specific criteria through which learning will be assessed (outcomes/success criteria);
> assessment approaches (*What* will you assess? *Who* will you assess? *How* will you assess?);
> resources needed.

Trainees often find it difficult to distinguish between success criteria and learning objectives. It is vital that you understand the difference between these terms (see below). Broad learning objectives and a lack of clarity in success criteria often result in learning and assessment that lack focus.

Writing detailed lesson plans helps you to mentally rehearse the lesson content before teaching it. You may not need to refer to the plan much once you have written it because the process of planning has enabled you to think through the lesson clearly. As well as being an aide-memoire for you, the lesson plan also serves to demonstrate to your mentor(s) and tutor(s) that you have given your lessons serious consideration. In short, lesson plans help to demonstrate your commitment to teaching as a profession.

Learning objectives

The learning objectives state what the pupils are going to learn. You can use the statements from the Programmes of Study in the National Curriculum but sometimes it may be necessary to break them down further in order to make them more focused. In literacy and numeracy, use the learning objectives in the revised frameworks for literacy and numeracy, but also include the statements from the National Curriculum Programmes of Study.

A suitable learning objective in English for children in Year 1 is presented below.

The children will be taught:

> to convey information and ideas in simple non-narrative forms.

This has been taken from the appropriate curricular framework for children in KS1.

Learning objectives for children in the EYFS can be taken from the Development Matters statements in the EYFS framework. One example is presented below.

The children will be taught:

> to attempt writing for various purposes using features of different forms such as labels.

Success criteria

Identify what knowledge, skills or understanding you want the children to know, do or understand by the end of the lesson in order to achieve the learning objective. The use of simple 'I can' statements can help children to recognise what they need to be able to know, understand or do in order to be successful.

The example below illustrates this.

Learning objective: The children will be taught:

> to convey information and ideas in simple non-narrative forms.

Success criteria:

> I can think of and say a sentence.
> I can write all the words in the order that I have said them in a sentence.
> I have left spaces between all the words I have written.

These should be SMART targets (specific, measurable, achievable, realistic and timed). In the above example the success criteria are differentiated to ensure that the learning of all children within a group or class is measurable. These criteria help children to recognise their own achievements, no matter how small. This example also demonstrates that children must complete several steps in learning to fully meet one learning objective.

The success criteria are the expected outcomes in terms of what you want the pupils to know or to be able to do by the end of the lesson. They break down the learning objective into more measurable outcomes. These specific criteria help your learners to understand what success looks like.

Success criteria *must* be differentiated for different abilities. You will assess pupils at the end of the lesson against the success criteria.

Taking ownership of your planning

To teach lessons effectively you need to have ownership of your planning. It is incredibly difficult to teach from a plan produced by someone else. You will teach better when you have thought the lesson through carefully.

Using assessment information to drive your planning

The assess–plan–teach cycle is fundamental to effective teaching. Before you begin the planning process you need to establish what your learners already know and can do. Organised trainees produce detailed medium-term and weekly plans to support their teaching. However, what you ultimately end up teaching in a specific lesson will depend on how your learners have responded in a previous lesson. You may have planned a series of lessons on addition in mathematics but specific misconceptions may arise during the first lesson. Your subsequent lesson plan should take account of how your learners have responded in the previous lesson. Individual children or groups may need some reinforcement before moving onto the next concept. Misconceptions may need to be addressed with individuals and groups of children before you can move onto the next aspect of learning. Additionally some children may make faster progress than initially anticipated. Consequently you will need to plan further challenges for these children. It is important for you to remember that you should focus on the quality of children's learning rather than coverage of specific learning objectives. It is not the amount you cover that is important; it is children's understanding that should be your prime focus. We recommend that trainees take a flexible approach to lesson planning. It can be detrimental to adhere to plans when you identify during your teaching that amendments would enhance learning.

Annotating your plans

We recommend that you plan a series of lessons (particularly in mathematics or English) to show the intended coverage during the week. This is especially important in situations where you are responsible for teaching a specific subject each day. This will enable you to think about how each group of learners will progress during the week. Before you start each teaching week you should have some outline planning in place. However, it is important for you to remember that your plans are not set in stone and should be flexible enough to cater for children's emerging learning needs during the week. At the end of each teaching day you should annotate your planning in pencil to show ways in which you have had to adapt the intended coverage to take account of your day-to-day formative assessments. Your annotations should focus on children's learning rather than your teaching and these should include simple words and phrases. Medium-term plans can also be annotated to show how the content has had to change in order to respond to children's emerging learning needs.

The aim of annotating your plans is to show that your planning file is a working document. Trainees often like their files to look good and they resist writing annotations on plans as they do not like to deface their work. However, it is these annotations which help to demonstrate that you are using formative assessment effectively and being responsive to children's immediate needs.

Planning for progression

Your planning should evidence your ability to plan for progression in children's learning. Progression is not something that happens naturally; it needs to be planned for. However, before you can plan for progression in learning you need adequate subject knowledge. You need to understand the progression sequence within specific strands of learning, for example in fractions, addition, shape and space, reading (phonics and comprehension), writing, speaking and listening, and scientific investigation. This is not an exhaustive list but thinking about progression within these aspects of learning will be a very good starting point.

Without this subject knowledge you will not be able to plan to advance learning and you will not be able to differentiate effectively to cater for the diverse learning needs of children in your class. Curricular frameworks are a good place to start when thinking about progression as they identify progression sequences within specific strands of learning. Your mentors should be able to identify clearly how you plan for whole classes, groups and individuals to make progress during a half term, within a week and within a lesson.

When you produce your medium-term plans think carefully about how you will enable learners to make progress from their starting points. If you are planning half a term's work on electricity you need to think carefully about how you will develop children's knowledge, skills and understanding over five, six or seven weeks. Within your outline weekly plans you need to identify how children will progress within focused units of work. Finally you need to think about progression within lessons. This is best achieved through:

> establishing what learners already know and can do;
> chunking the lesson into a series of smaller parts and within each part plan to develop children's knowledge, skills and understanding;
> making clear to children what you expect them to be able to achieve by the end of the lesson;
> teaching lessons which have good pace.

Using a range of teaching approaches

In your lessons you should aim to use a range of strategies to cater for the diverse learning styles of children in your class. Trainees should use the following strategies throughout lessons.

> Visual strategies: use plenty of visual images to support your teaching, and demonstrate tasks to children and include modelling. Examples of visual images include artefacts, pictures, photographs, subject-related resources and natural objects.
> Auditory strategies: use clear, straightforward instructions and explanations as well as audio recordings. It is best if audio strategies are also combined with visual strategies.
> Kinaesthetic strategies: young children generally learn through rich first-hand experiences. Build in opportunities for children to learn in this way.

Make your lessons interactive. Try to use teaching approaches which enable all learners to participate in the learning experience. Some interactive strategies are as follows:

> using small whiteboards so that learners can all show you their responses;
> asking children to use the interactive whiteboard;

> asking children to come out and explain/demonstrate;
> using talk partners or thinking in pairs;
> playing games with the whole class during whole-class sessions;
> washing line activities for sequencing work – asking children to sequence a set of cards.

Some useful websites to support interactive teaching are listed at the end of this chapter.

Case study

A second year trainee teacher was teaching a class of Year 1 pupils. The children were developing their understanding of toys from the past. The trainee had carefully considered a creative approach to his teaching to ensure that the children were motivated and engaged in the lesson. Resources to support the lesson were imaginative and stimulating. The trainee had created a magic wardrobe which contained a range of toys from the past. The children were required to place their hands inside the wardrobe, focusing on one item. They were asked to describe what they could feel behind the wardrobe curtain and verbalise their ideas to the rest of the group. Other children in the group were asked to engage in the learning by posing questions to discover more about the toy. The child then revealed the toy by taking it from the wardrobe and the group was given the opportunity to further explore the object.

Reflection

> How would you develop this lesson?
> Can you think of other innovative ways to introduce children to similar themes?

Planning your questions

It is important to plan your questions carefully before you teach a lesson. This strategy will encourage your learners to develop their thinking skills and foster pupil participation in the lesson. Try to ask open rather than closed questions, for example: *Tell me how you worked that out? What sort of character was the wolf in that story? Can we think of a better word to use?*

Remember to give the children thinking time and thinking in pairs is often a useful strategy for developing peer support. Include key questions on your lesson plans, although other questions will inevitably arise during the lesson. Plan a range of simple and more complex questions to cater for the diverse range of abilities in your class. It is also important that you integrate opportunities for allowing the children in your class to ask their own questions.

Planning for differentiation

Before you can effectively differentiate the tasks you provide the children with you need to establish precisely what different groups or learners need to know and be able to do. You will usually need different learning outcomes for different groups of learners. For learners with additional and different needs (including gifted children) you will need to identify individual learning outcomes to meet their needs. To identify appropriate learning outcomes you need to use your assessments of children's prior knowledge, skills and understanding as well as your knowledge of specific misconceptions which learners may have. You also need to understand progression sequences within specific subjects or aspects of learning. You need to build on what learners already know and can do in order to develop the learning further. Accurate differentiation therefore depends on accurate assessments and accurate subject knowledge.

When extending children's learning beyond that planned in a lesson, it is essential that you do not fall into the trap of merely providing them with more of the same diet. You will need to consider the next step in their learning and provide support and opportunities for them to demonstrate achievement at the next level.

Reflection

Children have been learning in a practical context about pairs of numbers that make 10 and have demonstrated a clear understanding. They know that if they have 6 insects on a leaf they must add 4 more to total 10 through counting on using the practical equipment. They can do this for all pairs of numbers that make 10.

> Discuss with a talk partner the ways in which the learning can now be extended. Do not automatically assume that the next step is to merely extend the number range.

Planning from children's interests

You should seek opportunities to plan learning experiences which relate to children's own interests. This will increase levels of motivation and participation within lessons. Many practitioners in the EYFS are experts in planning learning around children's interests. Think carefully about how you can use children's interests in reading, writing and mathematics as a context for learning. If children are interested in a specific sport this could form the basis for work in data handling. Interests in television characters or super-hero characters could form the focus for children's writing. When starting topics take the opportunity for children to tell you what they already know and then ask them what they would like to find out further. Their questions could be written onto a class mind map which can be revisited at frequent intervals.

Case study

Fran was undertaking her final teaching placement in a Year 1 class. She found it particularly difficult to plan for progression in children's learning. Her mentor had already expressed concerns that the children appeared to be making little progress after the first week of Fran's placement. Fran decided to take responsibility for her own professional development. She researched into the strands of progression within specific aspects of learning, using the Primary Framework. This enabled her to select learning objectives from higher or lower stages within specific strands, thus aiding differentiation. Additionally Fran asked her class mentor for prior assessments of children's learning. She then used the APP materials from the National Strategies to identify significant 'next steps' for individuals and groups of learners. Fran became skilled at identifying differentiated learning outcomes for different groups of learners using the progression strands and the APP materials. After four weeks the vast majority of children had made rapid progress. Fran then carried out detailed assessments of the learners whose progress was slower. She used her knowledge of these children to plan significant next steps to enable them to make more rapid progress. Fran identified specific success criteria for these individual learners on her planning and then she planned appropriate differentiated activities to address these learning outcomes. By the end of the placement all the learners had made good progress.

Reflection

> What do you think 'significant next steps' are and how can you identify these?
> How can you identify specific learning outcomes (success criteria) for individuals and groups of learners?
> How do differentiated learning outcomes help to secure good rates of progress?

Case study

Paul was placed in a school with parallel classes. There were two Year 5 teachers, each with a class, and two teaching assistants. Paul was keen to involve the whole team in the planning process. He consulted his mentor about the possibility of holding a weekly planning meeting to ensure parity of curriculum coverage for both of the classes. He also wanted the teaching assistants to contribute to the planning process. Both teaching assistants supported groups of learners with special educational needs. Paul encouraged them to suggest ways in which activities might be differentiated to meet the needs of these learners.

Reflection

> Why is team planning so important?
> How can you create the time for team planning?
> How would you overcome the difficulties of engaging qualified professionals in such professional dialogue, given that you are a trainee?

Professional development

Planning systems vary greatly from school to school in terms of content and complexity. Many head teachers continue to impose whole-school systems for planning, even though this is against current advice. However, in some schools individual teachers are offered the freedom to develop their own planning systems. If you have the opportunity to develop flexible approaches to planning we recommend that you do not do this in isolation. A discussion with tutors and mentors would be beneficial. Additionally share practices from other schools with your peers. Consider the expectations of your ITT provider and your school when developing your own approaches to planning. It is unlikely that one planning proforma will effectively meet your entire needs. Be prepared to combine the best elements from a range of examples in creating your own proformas. Adaptations may still be necessary.

Link to research

Bloom's Taxonomy (Hayes, 2009: 72–73) identifies specific categories of learning. The bottom layer represents a basic level of learning and the top level identifies the most complex skill. The ability to understand and apply knowledge is a more demanding skill than the ability to recall knowledge. You can use this model to extend learning for your more able learners. It is also a useful model to help you differentiate your questions.

Further reading

Medwell, J. (2007) *Successful Teaching Placement: Primary and Early Years*. Exeter: Learning Matters.
This text provides a comprehensive overview of all the challenges and issues associated with trainee teaching placements.

Useful websites

nationalstrategies.standards.dcsf.gov.uk/primary/primaryframework
This site provides information on units of work for planning literacy and mathematics.

numeracy.cumbriagridforlearning.org.uk/index.php?category_id=3
The Cumbria Grid for Learning provides useful information on medium-term planning and links to teaching resources.

www.topmarks.co.uk/interactive.aspx
www.bbc.co.uk
These sites provide a range of resources to support interactive teaching.

4

Outstanding teaching

This chapter covers

This chapter addresses the elements of an outstanding lesson. We focus on the importance of learner progress during lessons and strategies to support learners to reflect upon and articulate their own learning. We emphasise the importance of capturing the interest of learners and building a strong rapport with them. Additionally we explore strategies for monitoring learners' progress in lessons and stress the importance of teacher subject knowledge.

According to Ofsted outstanding trainees are able to demonstrate the following criteria in lessons. Outstanding trainees are able to:

> teach lessons that are mostly good, and often show characteristics of outstanding lessons;
> ensure that all learners make progress so that they fully achieve the challenging intended learning outcomes;
> teach learners to be able to explain how the teaching helped them to make progress;
> teach lessons that invariably capture the interest of learners, are inclusive of all learners, and feature debate between learners and between learners and the teacher;
> have a rapport with learners;
> monitor learners' progress to evaluate quickly how well they are learning so that they can change the approach during the lesson if necessary, and provide detailed feedback and targets to individual learners that are focused well to ensure further progress;

> demonstrate the ability to apply their own depth of subject knowledge to support learners in acquiring understanding and skills, often showing understanding, through application of a range of different approaches to ensure that all learners make the expected progress;
> demonstrate flexibility and adaptability by changing pace, approach and teaching method in a lesson in response to what learners say and do;
> make links with other aspects of learners' development and under-standing (for example, linking to work in other subjects);
> fully exploit possibilities to promote learners' understanding and appre-ciation of social and cultural diversity. (2009: 29)

This chapter provides you with guidance on how you might demonstrate these criteria during your teaching placements.

Teaching good and outstanding lessons

Outstanding trainees are consistently able to teach *good* lessons and they are often able to demonstrate *characteristics* of outstanding lessons. It is important to emphasise that you are not expected to consistently teach outstanding les-sons in order to be graded as outstanding overall. The important word within the Ofsted criteria is 'characteristics'. To be outstanding by the end of your pro-fessional training the vast majority of your lessons will need to be at least good and many of your lessons will have outstanding features. Some of your lessons may well have been outstanding. The key to being graded as an outstanding trainee lies in demonstrating that you have the *potential* to be an outstanding teacher.

You will, nevertheless, aspire to teach outstanding lessons. Outstanding lessons generally demonstrate the following characteristics.

> Planning is of a very high standard and resources are of an excellent quality.
> A wide range of teaching strategies are used.
> Very good subject knowledge is demonstrated with very clear explanations/ excellent modelling.
> All pupils learn at a substantial pace, they thrive and all learners make excep-tionally good progress.
> All pupils enjoy the lesson and are fully immersed. Pupil participation by all pupils is consistent throughout the lesson.
> Work is very well matched to the learners' needs (through prior assessment) and *all* learners are eager to respond to the challenges.

> ICT is used very effectively if appropriate.
> Classroom management is very effective and relationships are very strong. There is a very positive climate, which generates excellent behaviour.
> A wide range of assessment strategies are employed.
> Teaching is exemplary; it is imaginative and engages the learners.
> Support staff are effectively and creatively deployed to support learning.

It is important to emphasise that you will need to demonstrate the majority of these characteristics in order for your lessons to be graded outstanding. Outstanding lessons are those in which all learners make substantial progress throughout the lesson and the teaching and tasks are suitably pitched so that all learners are challenged. You therefore need to ensure that the learning outcomes for groups and individual learners are informed by accurate identification of pupils' next steps in learning. Your prior assessments of learners' needs should consequently inform the planning process.

Vygotsky's notion of the ZPD refers to the distance between a child's actual level of development and their proximal (potential) development, which can be achieved through the support of a more able other. This can be a teacher, peer, parent or other adult. Learning therefore needs to take place within this zone, rather than at the level which the child has already reached. Tasks consequently need to be pitched at a level above the child's existing level of development, but the level of differentiation should also take into account a child's potential when the child is provided with support and guidance. Tasks should neither be too easy nor too difficult. This will ensure that the child is appropriately challenged. The model assumes that the child can be *supported* to achieve their potential level of development. This model has implications for the role of teachers, parents, other adults and peers in supporting a child through their zone. Once the child has been supported through their ZPD, the level of support can gradually be withdrawn as they will be able to operate independently. This is often referred to as 'scaffolding'. Scaffolding provides a temporary support until a child can operate independently at a higher level.

In evaluating whether lessons are outstanding, learner progress is fundamental and children need to move through their respective ZPDs. By the end of the lesson there needs to be evidence of *development*, either in knowledge, skills and understanding or in attitudes. Accurate prior assessment can determine actual levels of development but the identification of challenging learning outcomes (next steps) needs to be based on what each child/group can achieve with support.

Vygotsky's theoretical model assumes that to move through the zone, learners will need to be challenged but also supported in the process. This has implications for the ways in which learners are supported during the lesson in order to make the expected levels of progress. Children can be supported by the teacher, teaching assistant or by their peers. Karpov (2005) has emphasised that joint activity with adults is essential to move children through the ZPD. It is important to work *with* children in a shared activity rather than simply using verbal mediation. Teacher and support staff can initially use verbal mediation to explain and model procedures followed by joint activity with the child whereby the procedure is practised. The adult can guide the child and withdraw support when the child demonstrates mastery (Goswami and Bryant, 2010).

The model reminds teachers of the importance of ensuring that all learners are realistically challenged and consequently the lesson/tasks should not be too easy or too difficult. At some points in the lesson, children may find aspects of the learning challenging, but through support they eventually master the learning and consequently reach a new developmental level. Learning outcomes should be framed from your own knowledge of what your learners are capable of. Lessons which consolidate what learners already know and can do are unlikely to be outstanding. All learners should be supported to achieve their potential development. Teachers must not focus solely on learners at lower stages of development.

Collaborative learning

Socio-cultural theory emphasises how knowledge is a product of social interactions. This has implications for developing collaborative work within lessons. Collaborative work provides a vehicle for the development of children's speaking and listening skills. However, it is important to recognise that children will not automatically be able to work collaboratively. The skills of task allocation, turn taking, questioning, sharing, listening and valuing the contributions of others need to be taught explicitly before children will benefit from collaborative work. Once these skills are established, collaborative work can become a vehicle for effective learning. The PACE Project (Pollard and Triggs, 2000) found that children generally prefer to work with friends. However, research has also found that children recognise that working with friends can be a distraction and that non-friendship grouping can sometimes be more beneficial (Flutter and Rudduck, 2004).

Vygotsky (1962; 1978) emphasised the role of language in developing children's thinking. This has implications for the quality of verbal interactions between adults and children and between learners.

In outstanding lessons there will be evidence of clear purposes for learning. Children need to have a clear understanding of the reasons for engaging with given tasks. In general, lessons taught in isolation and out of context will lack purpose. Purposeful lessons are meaningful to children. A good example of this is when children are asked to write. They need to know the intended purpose of the writing task and the audience it is aimed at. When you introduce lessons to children, you need to explain clearly the relevance of specific aspects of learning. It is important that you explain clearly to children why they are being asked to develop new skills. A lesson on measurement lacks purpose if children cannot identify its relevance to everyday contexts. Children therefore need frequent opportunities to use their knowledge and skills in meaningful situations. Once children have developed the skills associated with 'measurement' in mathematics, they need opportunities to use this skill for specific purposes. Examples of these could include:

> making models or creating recipes in design and technology;
> reading scales in science;
> calculating distances between given points on maps and plans in geography.

Essentially the reasons for using this skill constitute the 'bigger picture' and lessons can be made more purposeful if children know how the specific lesson contributes to the wider context of learning. At the beginning of lessons it is important that you make the purposes of the learning explicit to the children by making links to this wider context where possible.

During the planning process you should give careful consideration to the ways in which you can engage children in learning within imaginative contexts. These contexts should aim to inspire learners and capture their interest. The following case study illustrates the use of such contexts in the teaching and learning process.

Case study

Stefan was undertaking his final teaching placement in a Year 2 class in a large infant school. The school was following a whole-school theme related to 'space'. Stefan wanted to develop the children's scientific enquiry skills in relation to their understanding of changes in materials. To facilitate learning he developed an imaginative lesson which linked to the whole-school theme. The children were seated in a circle at the start of the lesson. There was a knock at the door and the teaching assistant entered the classroom with a huge parcel which had just

(Continued)

(Continued)

arrived at the school by special delivery. This created an atmosphere of suspense. Stefan encouraged the children to guess what might be in the parcel. He drew the children's attention to the postage stamp, which was marked 'Pluto'. Excitedly the children opened the package to reveal a freezer box containing four large eggs made out of ice. Inside the parcel there was a letter addressed to the children. The letter explained that the eggs had been sent from Pluto and that inside each egg there was a task for the children to complete. The letter continued by challenging the children to retrieve the messages as quickly as possible by finding the most effective way of melting the eggs. The letter requested that the children should reply, explaining the ways in which they had met the challenge.

The teacher divided the children into four groups. The groups were each supported by an adult, who had been carefully briefed before the lesson began. The children were engaged in discussions, with the supporting adults, about the ways in which the eggs could be melted quickly, how they would compare results from each group as well as the best ways of recording and presenting the information. The result of these discussions was that one group decided to cover the egg in newspaper, another group used foil, the third group used woollen material and the fourth group used bubble wrap. At a fixed point in time the eggs were removed from the freezer box and the children began their investigations. Throughout the morning, the children wrote their replies to Pluto and at given points observed and recorded, in tables and graphs, the ongoing results of their experiments. At the end of the morning the groups compared their findings and identified the most effective material used to melt the egg. The messages inside the eggs were retrieved by each group. The messages led into additional learning related to writing. This ensured that children make links in their learning and that all learning had a clear purpose.

Reflection

> How did Stefan engage the learners?
> How did Stefan create clear purposes for learning?
> How did Stefan link learning from different curriculum areas?
> Consider how you could further develop links with other curriculum areas.

Enquiry-based learning

In outstanding lessons trainee teachers will plan for enquiry-based learning opportunities. This involves learners in a process of taking ownership of their own learning through:

> independent research/investigation about topics they are studying;
> problem-solving tasks;
> using and applying learning from one context to another, for example applying taught skills in mathematics to an enterprise project;
> play-based learning.

In these lessons learners will be given opportunities to take responsibility for their own learning. The use of enquiry-based approaches to learning enables children to learn through:

> first-hand experience;
> collaborative learning – children scaffolding each others' learning;
> access to a range of resources, including electronic resources, pictures, photographs, artefacts and books;
> a range of learning styles – visual, auditory and kinaesthetic.

Case study

Julie was teaching a Year 4 class about 'life in Victorian times'. In the first lesson she asked the children to contribute to a class 'mind map' where she recorded facts that they already knew related to life in Victorian times. Julie then asked the children to identify questions relating to aspects that they did not know. These questions were recorded on the mind map and supported Julie in planning a series of lessons that effectively met the needs of the children. Julie subsequently divided the class into five groups. Each group of 'detectives' was asked to research information relating to a specific aspect of Victorian life. The children used books, electronic resources, artefacts, pictures, photographs and DVD footage to help them in their research. Together Julie and the children formulated clear success criteria for the subsequent activities.

Following the research, each group worked collaboratively to plan a group presentation to disseminate their findings. The presentations used a range of formats, including:

> poster presentations;
> films;
> PowerPoint presentations;
> interactive displays.

(Continued)

(Continued)

In addition to the presentation Julie asked each group to produce an information booklet for their peers. The class then became involved in peer assessment. The children were asked to assess both the presentation and the booklets and each group was provided with peer feedback on their work.

Reflection

> How did Julie empower the children to take responsibility for their own learning?
> What links were made to other curriculum areas?
> How could further links to other curriculum areas have been made?
> How did Julie plan for purposeful learning?

In outstanding lessons children will be highly motivated to extend their own learning through asking their own questions. According to Cremin (2009) creative teachers employ careful questioning to develop children's thinking and enquiry skills. She argues that children should be encouraged to share their own questions. Asking children to think of questions with a talk partner is a useful strategy for encouraging learners to generate their own questions. Talented trainee teachers provide children with opportunities to find answers to these questions for themselves. Outstanding trainee teachers will have the confidence to acknowledge to children that they do not hold the answer to every question and will work alongside the children to support them in finding answers to questions.

As previously mentioned in Chapter 1, trainee teachers should embrace unforeseen opportunities to enhance children's learning. This is effectively illustrated in the following case study.

Case study

Alice was in the third week of her second placement in a Foundation Stage classroom. Through break time she was preparing activities for the subsequent session. At the end of the break time Alice was greeted by a class of lively and excited children. Their excitement stemmed from the discovery of a hedgehog on the school field. The children eagerly asked a wide range of questions. In response to their excitement Alice made a professional decision to delay the delivery of the lesson she had planned and took the children back to the field to observe the hedgehog. The children were actively encouraged to pursue their questioning. These questions were answered by Alice, peers and observations of the hedgehog. Alice provided the children with digital cameras and movie makers to record the hedgehog and the children were encouraged to produce drawings of the hedgehog. Following this session the children were provided with further opportunities to find out about hedgehogs during independent and supported learning activities reflecting a range of curriculum areas.

Reflection

> Do you think Alice was right to delay her planned lesson?
> How can you capitalise on children's interests in developing the wider learning environment?

Ensuring that learners make progress

Ensuring that your learners make progress in their learning is a key part of being an effective trainee teacher. Schools are accountable to parents, carers, local authorities, the government and children. All schools are required to demonstrate how well they enable learners to make progress and consequently progress has to be monitored on a term-by-term and yearly basis.

Learner progress within lessons is fundamental. It involves:

> identifying what learners already know and can do;
> identifying significant 'next steps' that will move learning on so that children can achieve key milestones;
> supporting learners to achieve their next steps.

Effective assessment is central to learner progress. In lessons you will need to monitor whether children are achieving the intended learning outcomes. You will need to observe children carefully and identify emerging misconceptions. You will then need to support children through their misconceptions. This approach is an application of Vygotsky's ZPD and scaffolding theory. Additionally you will need to observe within lessons those individuals or groups of learners who need further challenge. Children may master a learning outcome more quickly than you expected and you will need to implement an extension activity to enable them to make further progress within a lesson.

Identifying challenging intended learning outcomes is also fundamental to aiding learner progress. You will need to identify significant 'next steps' for your learners, based on accurate prior assessments. These next steps should take account of nationally expected levels of attainment. You will therefore need to have a good knowledge and understanding of what learners need to be able to do to move from one level/stage of development to another. The APP materials produced by the National Strategies are useful in identifying specific assessment foci at different levels of attainment. However, you should spend some time becoming familiar with the assessment systems used in your school to help you identify these significant targets for your learners.

Your understanding of progression in specific strands of learning (reading, writing, calculations, number, shape, fractions, for example) needs to be secure before you can start to plan appropriate lessons to meet the needs of your learners. The *Primary Framework for Literacy and Mathematics* (DfES, 2006) provides helpful guidance on progression within specific strands of learning. You need to read this in conjunction with the APP materials to enable you to develop an understanding of how progression is related to national expected levels of attainment. If you are working in the EYFS the Foundation Stage framework (DfES, 2007) identifies clear strands of progression in all areas of learning. For trainees working in Reception classes, this document should be read in conjunction with the EYFS profile (QCA, 2008) which identifies significant steps which children need to take.

As a trainee teacher a useful starting point will be to collect prior assessments for the whole class before starting your placement. This statistical information should be available in school and you can use this data to plan for progression in pupils' learning. This is a key professional competency for QTS. However, it is important to remember that no single document will provide you with all the information you need to plan for progression in learning. You will be required to draw together information from a range of documentation and this is no easy task. Additionally no commercially available planning can be finely tuned to meet the needs of your learners. Outstanding trainees have an intuitive knowledge of the needs of individuals and groups of learners and this, combined with a knowledge of the significant next steps which pupils need to take and strands of progression within subjects, will make it possible for you to plan lessons which enable your learners to make progress.

Enabling learners to articulate their learning

Your learners should be able to articulate what they have 'learnt' during a lesson. This is fundamentally different to articulating what they have 'done', which is task orientated. Pupils will find this difficult if they do not know what the intended learning outcomes of the lesson were. This has implications for the way in which you share learning outcomes with children. During the lesson you need to keep reminding your learners about the intended learning outcomes and you need to revisit these in the plenary. You need to give the children opportunities to articulate the new learning at various points in the lesson and this may need to be planned for. The use of child-friendly *I can* statements will enable children to understand and articulate their learning.

Capturing learners' interest

The ability to capture the interest of your learners at the beginning of lessons is fundamental to successful teaching. To achieve this you will need to think carefully about the resources you use as stimuli for your lessons. Depending on the lesson you could capture learners' interest through the use of puppets, stories (read or told), interesting objects/artefacts, pictures, photographs, a display, a piece of music, a poem or a specific piece of software on the interactive whiteboard. Additionally you could capture learners' interest through the use of visiting speakers or through the use of drama at the beginning of lessons. We have observed some very effective trainees teaching in role by dressing up as characters as a stimulus for literacy or history lessons. The limits to innovative ways of engaging learners are only constrained by the limits of your imagination! It is important, once you have initially captured the interest of your learners, to sustain their interest throughout the duration of the lesson. Try to vary the approaches you use for introducing lessons. One way of doing this is to develop a range of stimuli to capture the interest of the children as they may quickly lose interest if the same approaches are over-used. Even the most 'dry' content can be made interesting with a little bit of thought and imagination. If you fail to capture their interest at the start of the lesson, your lesson is unlikely to be successful.

Your learners should be eager and motivated to respond to the challenges in the lesson. In addition to the resources that you use, you should also think about creating a 'context' for the learning. Examples of such contexts include:

> asking children to work as 'scientists' for a specific company to investigate a problem;
> asking children to be 'history detectives' and search for clues about the past;
> asking children to be 'artists' responsible for creating a gallery.

Setting the context for learning can empower children to take responsibility, work carefully and methodically and produce high quality work. Giving children a purpose for their learning can help to capture their interest. If they know why they are being asked to complete a task, this will enable them to understand the reason for doing it.

Developing a rapport with your learners

Outstanding trainees are able to develop very positive relationships with their learners. Fundamentally you cannot expect children to respect you if you do not respect them.

This has implications for the way you address children. You should speak to them in a courteous manner and your communications with them should be overwhelmingly positive. Outstanding trainees develop excellent relationships with children. They are relaxed in children's company and they are able to have fun with them. As a trainee you must maintain your professional integrity with children. You are a professional and your role is to be a teacher, not to act as their 'best friend'. However, this does not mean that you cannot be friendly with children. Outstanding trainees are rarely authoritarian in nature. The skill is to ensure that your learners are aware of the boundaries and a useful strategy is to negotiate these with them at the start of your placement.

In lessons you should use positive language with children and never be tempted to use sarcasm. Behaviour management strategies should be positive and the classroom ethos should reflect a 'can do' attitude. Smile at the children and spend time listening to them. Try not to dominate your lessons with too much teacher talk. The balance should be in favour of child talk since the children should be working just as hard, if not harder than you! Laugh with the children but never at them! Emphasise what they can do, not what they cannot do and tell them frequently how lucky you are to be teaching them. This positive approach should empower the children to want to work hard for you because they know that you like them and have high expectations of them.

The days of *Don't smile before Christmas* are hopefully long forgotten. Effective teaching depends on the ability to establish effective relationships with your learners. Children are unlikely to learn if they feel frightened or intimidated. Children are unlikely to respect you if you do not demonstrate respect for them. Respect is mutual and not automatic. You should aim to guide children's learning through excellent adult–child interactions rather than controlling children's learning. Guiding learning places an onus on the teacher to work 'with' children rather than children 'working for' the teacher. Enabling children to see learning as a partnership between themselves and the teacher should facilitate the development of positive relationships.

Establishing a rapport with your learners needs to start on the first day that you meet them. During your lessons you will maintain a good rapport with your learners if:

> you emphasise their achievements and make them feel good about their responses and work;
> you emphasise a 'can-do' culture;
> you use positive behaviour management strategies;
> you protect learners' self-esteem;
> you develop non-hierarchical relationships with learners so that they do not feel intimidated by you;
> misconceptions are addressed in a positive way and seen as a vehicle for learning.

Developing a good rapport should enable you to have fun with your learners but to command their attention/respect when needed. Developing this balance should be a priority from the moment you start teaching your class.

Monitoring progress during a lesson

Assessment must not be a 'bolt-on' to teaching. Within lessons you should use a range of strategies to monitor the progress of your learners including:

> questioning;
> making notes or jottings;
> taking photographs of the learning taking place;
> contributions from support staff.

This will help you to 'evidence' the learning. We mentioned earlier in this chapter the importance of identifying misconceptions within lessons and providing children with additional support to enable them to make progress. One further approach which trainees should consider to help children address their misconceptions is the use of peer support. The use of peer scaffolding enables you to create a learning community where all learners are mutually supportive of each other. Very often children can explain things to each other in more effective ways than teachers can! Developing independence within your learners is also important. It is not appropriate, nor practical, for them always to depend on a teacher when they encounter problems. Developing an effective learning environment is just one way of facilitating independence in your learners. Your classroom environment might include access to word banks, number lines, dictionaries, worked examples (such as suggested ways of solving calculations in mathematics), ICT resources and learning walls to enable children to address their own misconceptions. These examples are not exhaustive and the resources which you choose to use to help learners develop independence will depend on the age range you are teaching and the teaching content.

Subject knowledge in lessons

Clearly you will need to research the subject matter/content of your lessons before you teach them. This will enable you to answer learners' questions confidently. However, the pedagogical knowledge associated with how to teach specific subjects is fundamental to effective teaching. You will need to employ a range of teaching approaches including:

> questioning;
> modelling/demonstrating;
> guided learning;
> enquiry-based learning;
> collaborative learning (peer–peer).

These approaches will allow children to access the knowledge, skills or understanding you are trying to teach. Outstanding trainees have a very good understanding of effective pedagogy in different subjects. For example, they may demonstrate a very secure understanding of the principles of scientific enquiry when teaching science or the nature of enquiry-based learning in history or geography. They may demonstrate a very good understanding of the principles of quality first teaching when teaching phonics and the recommended approach to structuring such a session. They may understand the elements of a shared writing or guided reading session and they may have a very good understanding of the principles of effective practice in the EYFS. Much of this knowledge will come through centre-based training and/or observation of effective teachers of different subjects.

📁   **Case study**

Carol was teaching a religious education lesson to a Year 2 class. The focus of the theme was Christianity. In the lesson Carol wanted the children to learn about places of worship in the Christian faith. Carol started the lesson by asking the children about their existing knowledge in relation to Christian worship. The points from the discussion were recorded onto a class mind map. She then told the children that the rest of the afternoon would be spent visiting the local church, where they would be met by the vicar. At the church the vicar engaged the children in a brief discussion about the role of the Church within their community. The children were then offered the opportunity to explore the church with a partner and were encouraged to generate questions in pairs which they could ask the vicar. The children were provided with digital cameras and were allowed to take photographs of artefacts and different parts of the church. The following day Carol recapped on the information that the children had gained and this was recorded on the mind map.

Reflection

> In what ways did Carol offer ownership of the learning to the children?
> Can you identify any links made to other curriculum areas?
> How could Carol have made further links to other curriculum areas?

Flexibility within a lesson

Trainees are often anxious about deviating from a lesson plan. However, some lessons do not go according to plan and learners may struggle to grasp the key knowledge or skills you are trying to teach. In this instance it is important to address specific misconceptions with individuals, groups or even the whole class. You may need to introduce further modelling/explanations that you had not planned in order to help your learners overcome their misconceptions. You should not see this as a failure on your part. Additionally learners may be reluctant to engage with a lesson. In this instance you should stop the lesson and do something different. You will need to spend some time evaluating what went wrong and why.

You should sometimes develop the flexibility to adapt the lesson in response to what your learners say and do. Children sometimes express their own ideas for pursuing their own learning and it is sometimes appropriate to capitalise on their interests and allow them to do this, providing it is related to the subject/content of the lesson. Knowing when children are employing task avoidance and when they have a genuine interest in pursuing an idea comes from your intuitive knowledge of your learners.

Linking subjects/areas of learning

Children's learning should enable them to make links to the 'bigger picture' and learning, where possible, should be linked. If learning is fragmented there is a danger that children will not understand the purpose of the tasks that they have been asked to undertake. During the planning stage, it is essential that you identify any cross-curricular links and that you exploit these links in your teaching.

If you are teaching a Year 3 class about the Romans as a history-focused topic and in ICT you are focusing on developing their ability to combine text with picture, it makes sense to plan a task which links the two foci. Therefore you might ask the children to produce an information booklet about the Romans using word processing software. Additionally this history-focused theme will also provide a context for literacy-based work. Thus, children could read non-fiction texts about the Romans in guided reading sessions and they could write simple non-chronological reports about life in Roman times. In this example, a theme on the Romans would provide a good vehicle for learning about symmetry and pattern in mathematics and this could also provide a stimulus for a theme in art and design. Children can explore symmetrical mosaic patterns and this can provide a rich context for learning in mathematics and art.

During a theme relating to 'the local environment' children can have opportunities to develop purposeful literacy skills. These could include:

> writing letters to the local council;
> creating tourist information booklets (linking literacy and ICT);
> producing posters about caring for the environment (linking literacy and ICT);
> presenting news reports about current events in the local area (speaking and listening);
> interviewing local people (speaking and listening; geography);
> visiting a local church (speaking and listening; religious education, history, ICT).

Additionally you should seek opportunities to make links with other areas of learning. Within the above example children could be asked to carry out traffic surveys to link with work in data handling in mathematics. Children could learn about the history or geography of the local area and could visit places of worship (linking with religious education).

However, whilst links between areas of the curriculum are important, it is vital that links are appropriate. At the planning stage you should consult with your mentor(s) about the appropriateness of different curriculum links. It is important to ensure progression and continuity within specific subjects and some links might not extend children's learning in a logical way. In the example above relating to the theme of the 'Romans,' it might be inappropriate to plan a series of mathematics lessons on symmetry and pattern if the class has already studied that theme, or if it is planned to be covered at a later point. Links can also be tentative.

Social and cultural diversity

The principles of inclusive education are outlined in the statutory framework for inclusion in the National Curriculum (DfEE, 1999). Schools consequently have a responsibility to create inclusive learning environments. In these environments:

> all learners feel happy;
> all learners have a sense of belonging;
> all learners feel valued and have a voice;
> all parents feel welcome;
> differences are celebrated and seen as positive and enriching.

As a trainee teacher you need to demonstrate a commitment to all of your learners, regardless of social background, culture, ethnicity, gender and disability. You need to demonstrate high expectations of every learner and to value each of them as individuals. Children's home backgrounds (social or cultural) can often enrich your teaching. You therefore need to think about ways in which you can draw on children's experiences to benefit your teaching.

It is important not to hold any prejudices about particular groups. All trainee teachers should consequently spend time reflecting on their own values and beliefs and make sure that any personal prejudices or stereotypes do not feature in their professional lives.

Your classroom environment can demonstrate a commitment to social and cultural diversity. Think carefully about the images you have on display or the books you have selected for use in the reading area. Do these materials depict a range of cultures, backgrounds and do they challenge stereotypes? Think about the resources that you use to support your teaching. Do your resources demonstrate a commitment to diversity? Do the labels, captions and notices on your displays reflect different languages? Carefully auditing your classroom environment is a useful starting point.

Think carefully about the way you treat parents and carers. Do you value all of them? Ensure that you do not formulate stereotypes about particular parents or carers and treat all of them with respect. Ensure that you do not make value judgements based on the clothes people are wearing and make sure that you do not perceive social class to be a barrier to educational potential or parental commitment to education.

Think carefully about how you will challenge value judgements made by children to each other. Outstanding trainees will operate within the school's discipline policy. Challenge sexist or racist comments or comments made about ability/disability. As a trainee teacher you are a role model. It is your responsibility to challenge discrimination and harassment and you need to be prepared to challenge 'home values' if these are prejudicial or discriminatory.

Exploit opportunities to develop learners' understandings of social and cultural diversity. Think carefully at the planning stage about how you can integrate opportunities for teaching children about diverse social and cultural backgrounds. However, be cautious not to create stereotypes in children's minds. Geography can be a useful vehicle through which you can introduce children to different cultures. However, not all people who live in third world countries are poor! Think carefully about places you can take children to educate them about different cultures or the resources that you can use to support your teaching (artefacts, pictures, photographs, puppets, electronic resources, food and clothing) to develop children's cultural awareness.

Ensure that children from different social classes do not feel excluded. Think carefully about the things you say to children. Do not assume that all children have access to computers, gardens and cars at home. Do not assume that all children are brought up in a 'traditional' family and are lucky enough to afford holidays abroad. Comments which demonstrate such assumptions can make some children feel excluded.

Ensure that you do not present the 'British' culture as the superior culture. Be sensitive to different cultural beliefs relating to food, clothing or religious beliefs. Children from travelling families will feel included if their culture is embraced and discussed. Try to create opportunities to introduce children to famous men and women from different social and cultural backgrounds in history and introduce children to art from different cultures.

This section has provided you with some ideas for addressing social and cultural diversity. At the planning stage you need to further consider opportunities for enhancing children's understanding of this important aspect of education.

Professional development

You are teaching a Year 2 class on your placement. The theme is 'Chocolate'. Using the National Curriculum and the *Primary Framework for Literacy and Mathematics*, identify the curriculum links which you could make.

Link to research

The PACE Project (Pollard and Triggs, 2000) found that children were motivated when they were praised and offered rewards for their work. However, other research suggests that children dislike repetition of tasks which merely consolidate prior learning and consequently fail to challenge them (Cullingford, 1991; Pollard and Triggs, 2000). Children need to see the value and purpose of their learning otherwise they become demotivated (Flutter and Rudduck, 2004).

Further reading

Miller, L. and Pound, L. (2010) *Theories and Approaches to Learning in the Early Years* (Critical Issues in the Early Years). London: Sage.
This text explores key thinkers in early years education and care, including Froebel and Montessori, and key approaches such as Steiner-Waldorf, High-Scope, Forest Schools and Te Whariki.

Wilson, A. (ed) (2009) *Creativity in Primary Education,* 2nd edn. Exeter: Learning Matters.
This text provides a comprehensive overview of creative teaching in different aspects of the primary curriculum.

Useful websites

outstanding-lessons.wikispaces.com/
This website provides useful practical advice on how to teach outstanding lessons.

www.teachers.tv/
This site will support you in reflecting on your own practice. The video clips provide opportunities for reflection and examples of outstanding practice in relation to different curriculum areas.

5

Assessment for learning

This chapter covers

This chapter reflects upon the principles of assessment for learning. It emphasises the link between the assessment process and its impact on planning. We argue that assessment should be a positive process which celebrates individual achievement. Additionally we argue that children should be active participants in the assessment process and should be involved in recognising their achievements as well as their future learning needs. The chapter demystifies the Ofsted criteria relating to assessment and provides practical advice to support trainees in demonstrating outstanding practices in assessment.

Assessment for learning

According to the Assessment Reform Group, assessment for learning is defined as:

> The process of seeking and interpreting evidence for use by learners and their teacher to decide where the learners are in their learning, where they need to go and how best to get there. (2002)

It is your responsibility to know your learners as individuals and to be able to identify their personal achievements, attainment and future learning needs. Assessment is an integral part of effective teaching and must be fully embedded in all aspects of your daily classroom practice. Your knowledge of each child's attainment will support you in the identification of focused targets for individuals and groups of learners. These targets must be focused and achievable to enable all learners to experience success. Assessment should be a constructive process which supports each child to move forward in their learning, thus building on current attainment. This must be an ongoing process which continually supports children in working towards the next identified goal for their learning. Formative assessment will support you in this process.

Medwell effectively summarises the purpose of assessment:

> You should know what the children can do, note what they have done and identify what they and you need to do next ... This is the role of assessment. (2007: 77)

Assessment for learning is formative in nature. It seeks to support your planning and your teaching as well as the children's learning. Each planned lesson should identify specific learning outcomes for individuals and groups of learners against which achievement is measured. Evidence of achievement against these learning outcomes will help you identify subsequent targets to support both individual and group learning. Alexander explains that:

> What this involves for teachers is best described as a cyclic process, in which they gather data about pupils' current understandings and skills by observation, careful questioning, gathering children's views and studying pupils' work, then interpret this information in relation to the lesson goals to decide the next steps in learning ... it requires that children as well as teachers have a clear idea of what they should be aiming for, thus enabling them to take part in assessing their work and gaining some independence in learning. (2010: 315)

Children should be actively engaged in the process of high quality formative assessment. Consequently you should ensure that your learners are fully involved in reviewing their own learning and they should be supported in developing the skills to identify future learning targets. With increasing maturity learners should be able to take responsibility for identifying their emerging learning needs.

Assessment for learning should be regarded as a key professional skill for all teachers. As you become increasingly familiar with the professional standards for QTS you will begin to understand how your ability to assess effectively impacts on your ability to achieve many of these standards. Effective assessment will ensure that you are able to identify the learning needs of individuals and groups of learners. These needs must be carefully considered as you plan for future learning. Focused planning will support the children in achieving their next steps. The ability to demonstrate high expectations of learners and provide personalised provision for individual learners is reliant on your understanding and effective implementation of the assessment process. Robust assessment systems enable you to evaluate the impact of your teaching on the progress of your learners. Effective assessment is underpinned by strong subject knowledge. This enables you to identify clear strands of progression within subjects, which inform immediate learning needs. Your ability to break down these steps into focused, measurable success criteria will ensure that assessment is sharp and teaching is differentiated to meet learners' needs. As you gain confidence and deepen your understanding you will begin to realise that professional attributes, knowledge and understanding, planning, teaching, learning and assessment are interlinked. Consequently an understanding of assessment is pivotal to fully achieving many standards for QTS.

Principles of assessment for learning

The Assessment Reform Group has identified ten principles to support effective assessment for learning. These should:

> be part of effective planning;
> focus on how students learn;
> be central to classroom practice;
> be a key professional skill;
> be sensitive and constructive;
> foster motivation;
> promote understanding of goals and criteria;
> help learners know how to improve;
> develop the capacity for self-assessment;
> recognise all educational achievement. (2002)

These principles ensure that all achievements are celebrated so that all learners should enjoy success and have a clear understanding of their achievements and immediate learning needs. Effective assessment for learning does not seek to label, categorise or compare learners with each other. It aims to effectively support and meet the needs of every child in every class.

Supporting learners to articulate their own progress

You should ensure that you frequently engage children in learning conversations to develop their ability to identify their achievements and fully engage in the assessment process. Through these learning conversations children should be able to articulate their own progress and developmental needs and with consistent, clear and effective support will become partners in the development of their own learning.

Outstanding trainees 'teach learners to be able to explain how the teaching helped them to make progress' (Ofsted, 2009: 29). In order to address this you should consider the following.

> Begin the lesson by ensuring that you are explicit about what the children will learn, what they will know and/or what they will be able to do by the end of the lesson.
> Be supportive and create a safe and secure learning environment in which the children have the confidence to acknowledge their learning needs to enable them to meet the intended learning outcomes. It is important that children are comfortable with identifying their needs as well as their achievements. It must be acceptable for children to admit their lack of understanding or ability at the start of a lesson and at any other point during the learning process.
> During the lesson frequently return to the intended learning outcomes. As the lesson progresses take time to stop briefly and check the children's understanding of what they have done. Take opportunities to revisit each stage of the lesson and remind the children what they learnt at each stage of the lesson and how each stage has built on their learning. During the lesson give the children opportunities to demonstrate their progress towards the learning outcomes by encouraging them to share their learning with the group, a peer and/or the teacher.
> At the end of a lesson again return to the intended learning outcomes. Ask the children to identify their achievements and to acknowledge their misconceptions. Encourage the children to independently *demonstrate* their understanding of the learning outcomes. Individuals may share their understanding with the group, with the teacher or with a partner. This is a fundamental opportunity for the teacher to assess individual achievements which should always be measured against the previously identified learning outcomes.
> At all stages of the lesson there are opportunities to assess learners' progress, particularly when the children are either demonstrating or explaining their learning to others. Capitalise on this as a crucial opportunity for formative assessment. Your assessments of children's achievements against the intended learning outcomes will support you in the identification of next steps in learning.

> Encourage children to either explain or demonstrate their achievements and understanding of their learning at all stages of a lesson. Be aware that children enjoy acknowledging success. Effective trainees must ensure that children can demonstrate their understanding and not just acknowledge it. Challenge learners to explain or demonstrate their understanding of the lesson outcomes.

Strategies for assessment

During your placement you will need to evidence progress, achievement and attainment. This can be done in a variety of ways as follows:

> observational assessment records;
> photographs – annotated to explain the context, what children said and did, the level of adult support and judgements against national performance criteria;
> video footage;
> digital recordings;
> samples of pupils' work;
> checklists and notes about children's achievement against intended learning outcomes;
> tests;
> sticky notes completed by you and other staff during lessons; this method is effective as children often demonstrate knowledge, understanding and skills in a range of contexts, for example number ordering may have been a focus during an adult-led mathematics activity but children may demonstrate their understanding of number ordering at other times.

The evidence can be stored electronically or in individual children's learning journals. This creates a picture of achievement, progress and attainment over time. During your placement you should carefully select samples of evidence which support judgements relating to significant achievement in specific subjects or areas of learning. If you are working in the EYFS the evidence selected should cover the six areas of learning as these are of equal importance.

> Personal, social and emotional development;
> Communication, language and literacy;
> Problem solving, reasoning and numeracy;
> Physical development;
> Creative development;
> Knowledge and understanding of the world.

If you are working in KS1 or KS2 there will be a minimum requirement to evidence achievement in the core subjects. As a trainee you will be required to keep assessment evidence for a specified number of children. You will also be required to demonstrate how you have made your judgements and how these judgements have impacted on subsequent planning.

It is important to emphasise that a single piece of evidence does not support judgements. You will need to see evidence that your learners are able to consistently demonstrate achievement during independent learning. Additionally it is pertinent to stress that a range of assessment evidence may be required to demonstrate a child's achievement of a specific learning outcome.

Identifying broader targets

Trainees must be aware of whole-school, class and group targets which will be part of the school's target setting policy. These targets are often broad in scope and provide learners with an ultimate goal over a given period of time. These targets are often linked to age-related national expectations. For example, to achieve an element of National Curriculum level 1 in writing, children must be able to demonstrate some awareness of the use of full stops and capital letters. This is the bigger target. Practitioners and learners should identify smaller steps which will lead to the ultimate achievement of the bigger target. In this example a series of smaller steps would be identified to support the child in achieving the broader target. These steps could include supporting a child to:

> independently recognise the difference between a sentence and a caption;
> think in sentences;
> articulate a sentence;
> write a sentence;
> check for the sense of a sentence by re-reading it;
> recognise the end of a sentence and begin to demarcate with a full stop;
> recognise the beginning of a sentence and begin to demarcate with a capital letter.

During your placement you must be familiar with the 'bigger picture' to ensure that you can support all learners in taking the significant steps towards achieving national age-related expectations. You should consider these targets at the planning stage and monitor individual achievement to enable you to move learning forward and to support children in subsequently achieving the broader target.

Linking assessment and planning

Outstanding trainees 'provide evidence of monitoring and recording learners' progress and how the outcomes are used in subsequent planning with a clear focus on groups and individual learners' (Ofsted, 2009: 32). Carefully consider developing and implementing manageable systems to record children's achievements against intended learning outcomes at the end of every lesson. All adults that support learning in the classroom must be comfortable and familiar with systems for recording evidence of progress. Each adult will be expected to contribute towards the assessment process and an important part of your role is to develop simple recording formats to support them in doing so.

A simple system is to list intended learning outcomes against children's names. Achievement can be recorded using a simple traffic light system (green = fully achieved; amber = partially achieved; red = not achieved). Some teachers use other symbols such as smiley/sad faces to record achievement. A tick/dash/cross system might also be used. Recording formats should also provide space for significant brief comments and there is no expectation to make detailed notes about each child. This is idealistic but impractical.

Completed recording formats of children's progress against intended learning outcomes are working documents. Use these, along with discussions with other adults, to identify emerging group and individual needs. Several learners within one group may have the same learning needs. However, it is commonplace, even within a small group, for learners to progress at different rates and consequently require different provision. Use your assessment record at the end of a lesson to identify learning outcomes in the next lesson for groups and individuals. You may need to consider whether the grouping arrangements are adequately meeting the needs of the learners or whether regrouping at this stage would be beneficial. Some children may require additional reinforcement of specific learning outcomes whilst others may have exceeded the expectations and will require carefully considered further challenges in their learning.

At the end of a lesson it is essential to revisit weekly plans and to annotate them to ensure that they adequately meet the needs of all children. Planning is a working document and must be responsive to the needs of learners. Consequently planning too far in advance is futile. A working document must demonstrate to your mentors and link tutors that you are reflective and meeting the needs of your learners. Resist the temptation to present your assessors with beautifully presented planning. They need to see your annotations as these demonstrate that you have used the assess–plan–review cycle.

Linking objectives, teaching approaches and assessment

According to Ofsted outstanding trainees 'demonstrate the clarity of links between learning objectives, teaching approaches and assessment strategies – "what I want learners to learn, how they will learn, and how I know that they have, what I will do next"' (2009: 32). The planning process must begin with the identification of learning objectives. These constitute broad statements of intent in relation to learning. These must then be broken down to meet the learning needs of individuals and groups of learners. The objectives and learning outcomes must match. Learning outcomes (or success criteria) will be used by you to measure achievement. These should enable learners and teachers and all adults to have a clear and shared understanding of achievement. Success criteria must be differentiated at group level as a minimum. However, it is often necessary to differentiate learning outcomes within a group at the level of the individual child.

The identification of clear learning outcomes for groups and individuals will effectively support robust differentiation. During the planning process it is vital that your starting point is the identification of clear learning outcomes. Once these have been clarified then, and only then, do you begin to plan and consider the tasks that will support all learners in achieving these outcomes. Outstanding trainees are able to design tasks which focus on the needs of all learners and address the planned learning outcomes. They design outcomes for groups and individuals which take account of prior assessment. This process effectively supports progress for all learners.

Sharing learning goals

Sharing learning intentions is a fundamental part of assessment for learning. Children need to be clear about the expected learning outcomes by the end of the lesson. Without a clear understanding of what they need to do to demonstrate success learners will be unable to identify their achievements or acknowledge a need for further support. Sharing expected learning outcomes lays firm foundations for engaging children in the self-assessment process because it focuses their understanding of what they need to do to succeed and it helps them to identify areas where they may have misconceptions.

Challenging learning outcomes in lessons

Outstanding trainees 'ensure that all learners make progress so that they fully achieve the challenging intended learning outcomes' (Ofsted, 2009: 29). Learning outcomes must be clearly identifiable small steps in learning. They must be achievable. Teaching must also focus on the intended learning outcomes. Throughout the lesson a range of strategies can be implemented to ensure that learners make progress.

> Open and closed questioning should be used during the lesson to check understanding. Good questioning can help to secure good progress.
> You will use observational assessment to identify whether learners are making progress or need further support.
> You may need to scaffold children's learning by providing further support to ensure progress. Teachers need to identify children's misconceptions in lessons and support children through these. For example, a child struggling to read simple consonant–vowel–consonant words many require further support in blending.
> Vary your approach: with good subject knowledge you will be able to quickly revisit and consolidate prior learning or extend learning and you may need to adapt your language and/or resources to ensure that learners make progress. Assessment is an ongoing process and will support you in knowing when to back-track or extend learning.
> Ensure that you engage the children in demonstrating and articulating their own progress within lessons.

There will be occasions during lessons when a child may not meet the outcomes of the lesson. You need to acknowledge this and provide additional intervention to help the child make further progress. You must first of all reflect on your own planning and teaching but you must also bear in mind that external factors could impact on learning. When a whole group of learners fail to meet the intended learning outcomes you must use this as an opportunity to reflect on your own practices. The following questions should facilitate this process of self-reflection.

> Were the learning outcomes appropriate for the needs of this group of learners?
> Were the intended learning outcomes made explicit to the children?
> Did the tasks and resources adequately support the intended learning outcomes?
> Was your own subject knowledge secure?

> Were the tasks appropriately differentiated to meet the needs of all learners within the group?
> Did you use too few or too many strategies to support learning?
> Were there any external factors which could have had a detrimental impact on learning?

Learner progress is fundamental and when planning for progression is effectively combined with stimulating and meaningful activities, this will engage and support all learners to achieve.

Monitoring progress and feedback

Outstanding trainees 'monitor learners' progress to evaluate quickly how well they are learning so that they can change the approach during the lesson if necessary, and provide detailed feedback and targets to individual learners that are focused well to ensure further progress' (Ofsted, 2009: 29). All lessons should be planned by you with careful consideration of current individual attainment and a clear identification of what you want learners to know and/or be able to do by the end of the lesson.

Learners within a small group could potentially start a lesson with the same learning needs. These will have been identified through accurate prior formative assessment. Some children may make rapid progress whilst others may require further consolidation to secure learning. Thus individual needs may begin to change during a lesson. It is important that you monitor these rates of progress and that through good subject knowledge you have the ability to support divergent learning needs. You may consider the following to support you in monitoring progress during a lesson.

> Record progress throughout the lesson on simple tracking sheets.
> Observe children closely to check that they are making good progress towards achieving the intended learning outcomes.
> Ensure that in the planning stages of the lesson you have considered and prepared extension activities as well as activities to consolidate learning for those who are making slower progress.
> Challenge children by extending their thinking skills through the use of open-ended questioning based on good subject knowledge.
> Create opportunities for children to apply their learning in everyday contexts.
> Support learners to make connections between areas of learning/subjects.

> Provide opportunities for peer support.
> Model and remodel strategies to clarify misconceptions.
> Simplify questioning and adapt your language to meet the needs of the learner.

Throughout the lesson ensure that you provide the learners with constructive, positive and focused feedback matched to the intended learning outcomes. Written feedback should identify achievements against the learning outcomes and communicate targets for future development. Effective feedback scaffolds children's learning so that learners understand how to achieve their targets and opportunities should be provided for learners to act on feedback. You should ensure that feedback is timely and where possible you should aim to provide learners with feedback within lessons. Verbal feedback is the most effective way of supporting younger children's progress. Ensure that you talk to children in lessons about their learning and communicate achievements as well as targets. You should avoid the use of vague feedback such as: *Well done. You have worked hard. Good try.* Feedback should always relate to the intended learning outcomes for an activity and should identify next steps in learning.

Discussing learners' progress with others

Outstanding trainees 'are able to discuss in detail individual learners' progress as well as attainment/achievement' (Ofsted, 2009: 34). You must know your learners as individuals. When considering attainment, achievement and progress we define the terms as follows.

> Achievement refers to a measure of what children know and can do at a given point in time.
> Progress is a measure of achievement, taking into account children's starting and exit achievements within a given time-scale. This could be over a period of a year, a term, half a term, a week or within a lesson.
> Attainment compares an individual's achievement with national standards.

A child could demonstrate good progress but poor attainment by rapidly building on prior learning but falling well short of nationally expected attainment. Another child could have a starting point just below nationally expected attainment for the child's age and could build slowly on prior learning to achieve the national expectations. Consequently this child would demonstrate slow progress but good attainment.

You should have a clear knowledge and understanding of prior achievement and progress. To have this you need to know:

> learners' starting points;
> current achievements;
> future learning needs;
> rates of progress taking into account starting points;
> current achievement compared with age-related national norms.

Outstanding trainees are able to reflect on ways of supporting children's progress further and enhancing their attainment. To facilitate this you must be sure of their understanding of the requirements to achieve national expectations. For trainees in the EYFS attainment is measured against the scale points of the EYFS profile. At the end of KS1 and KS2 attainment is measured against National Curriculum level descriptors in mathematics, English and science. You need to develop a secure knowledge and understanding of the expectations required to attain each sub-level in specific aspects of these core subjects. Without this knowledge you will be unable to support children in achieving national expectations.

At the end of KS2 there are statutory tests which measure learners' attainment against nationally expected norms. At the end of KS1 teacher assessment is pre-dominantly used to measure attainment against nationally expected norms. However, tests and tasks are still administered to support teacher assessments. At the end of the EYFS attainment is measured against the EYFS profile. All of these assessments are summative assessments in that they are a measure of learning (and attainment) at a fixed point in time. In order to maximise the chance of children achieving nationally expected outcomes, children are expected to sustain or exceed specified rates of progress at the end of each year. Outstanding trainees are able to make good use of national and school data to identify the needs of groups and individual learners in their endeavour to help children achieve national expectations. This is underpinned by a clear understanding of what learners must demonstrate to be able to achieve a given sub-level or scale point. However, all trainees must remember that progress is fundamental and that some learners will inevitably make good progress whilst demonstrating poor attainment. We argue that measures of progress are fundamentally more important indicators of teacher quality than measures of attainment.

Teacher assessment must be supported by evidence. Moderation of your judgements with colleagues is an essential process to ensure that your judgements are secure. Schools may have developed portfolios of assessment. These provide a benchmark against which you can compare your judgements. You must be prepared and able to substantiate all your judgements.

📁 **Case study: self-assessment**

Yasmin was a final year trainee working with a group of Year 2 children. She was keen to engage the children in the process of self-assessment. She devised a traffic light system using red, amber and green hoops. At the end of the lesson Yasmin reminded the children about the intended learning outcomes. She asked them to reflect upon their achievements and to identify these by placing their name in the hoops as follows.

> Green = I understand all the work I have done in the lesson today.
> Amber = I understand some of the work I have done today but need more help.
> Red = I do not understand the work I have done today.

Yasmin created opportunities during the plenary for the children to reflect on their decisions. She gave confident learners opportunities to demonstrate their achievement through questioning and simple tasks. She also asked less confident learners to articulate what they had found difficult and she clarified some key misconceptions. One of the children had indicated that he had achieved the learning outcomes. Through asking him to demonstrate this it became clear to Yasmin that he had encountered some misconceptions. She supported him sensitively to identify these and to acknowledge that he required further support.

Reflection

> What were the strengths of this system to address self-assessment?
> How could you enhance this process further?
> How can you ensure that self-assessment is accurate and supportive to children?

It is important to be aware that some children will follow their peers and claim success rather than face ridicule. For older children you may wish to consider systems which enable learners to identify their achievements or needs away from the gaze of their peers. This could involve children using a simple traffic light system on their own recorded work. However, it is crucial that children are sensitively supported to realise that their own misconceptions and misunderstandings are not seen as failure and that further support will always be available. All children should be confident in asking for further support and guidance, either in public or in private and the class ethos should be one of support rather than ridicule.

Involving parents and carers in assessment

Within the EYFS there is a requirement to engage parents and carers as contributors to the assessment process. The guidance for the EYFS profile states:

> Assessment must actively engage parents and/or other primary carers, the first educators of children, or it will offer an incomplete picture. Accurate assessment requires a two-way flow of information between setting(s) and home and reviews of the child's achievements should include those demonstrated at home. (QCA, 2008: 10)

If you are placed in a Foundation Stage setting you need to find out how practitioners involve parents and carers in the assessment process. Consider ways in which you could convey significant 'next steps' in learning to parents and carers and ways in which they could document evidence of achievement towards these steps and share them with you. For example, you could create a simple booklet entitled *My Next Steps*. It is vital that you share targets in relation to all six areas of learning. You may wish to work in partnership with parents and carers of a small group of children over half a term. You could initially review their child's achievements against the EYFS profile with them before identifying together new areas for further development. These could be related to the profile scale points. You could suggest ways in which parents or carers can support their children in achieving the identified targets. The booklet will provide an opportunity for sharing both dialogue and evidence and can contribute to the child's learning journal. This approach is based on the premise that learning takes places both at home and at school. This initiative could easily and effectively be adopted by trainees throughout the primary age phase. Be aware that some parents may over-exaggerate their child's attainment, wanting them to appear more able than they actually are. This highlights the importance of moderating assessment evidence.

Child voice in assessment

We have previously discussed the value of engaging children in frequent learning conversations. In these conversations you can discover children's perspectives about their learning, what they enjoy, what they find difficult and what further support they need. These conversations can be recorded and included in each child's assessment records. Children should regularly be encouraged to reflect on their learning and older children can document their reflections in writing or through a range of ICT applications. Hutchin (2007) identifies the need for children to reflect on their own development. Throughout effective assessment processes children should be familiar with their next steps in learning. Children must be empowered to be active participants in this process and be able to recognise their own achievements. With this understanding children can easily contribute evidence towards their own assessment records. Children of all ages can be encouraged to select the pieces of assessment evidence for inclusion in their portfolios/learning journals. Involving children in the assessment process provides them with a sense of pride and gives them ownership of the process. Malaguzzi (1993) discusses empowering children to document their learning and to reflect upon it. The inclusion of child voice within the assessment process is a principle of best practice and current policy agenda promotes child participation in all aspects of education.

Using assessment to evaluate your own teaching

In your lesson evaluations you should use your assessments to consider both the positive and negative impact of your teaching on the children's learning. Through the use of formative assessment you should be able to clearly identify the children who are making progress as well as those who are finding the work challenging. Consider the reasons for this and reflect upon the following.

> Are the children grouped appropriately?
> Do the intended learning outcomes match the current needs of all children?
> Are the learning outcomes clearly differentiated and based on prior achievement?
> Do the tasks support the learning outcomes for all children?
> Was the teaching effective?

If a group of children have not met the intended learning outcomes it is possible that either your teaching or the identified learning outcomes, or indeed both, have not suitably met the needs of the learners. Your assessments provide you with an opportunity to reflect on these important issues. It may be that only one child fails to meet the intended learning outcomes in a lesson. This may be a result of ineffective teaching or inappropriate learning outcomes. However, lack of progress could also be due to external factors or dispositions and attitudes towards learning. Your assessments and professional knowledge will support you in evaluating and understanding the reasons for this.

Case study: peer assessment

A small group of Year 5 learners were focusing on the use of connectives to enhance their writing. They were being supported by James, a trainee teacher, who was keen to develop strategies for peer assessment. At the beginning of the lesson James had discussed the use of connectives and he had asked the children to generate different examples of connectives which they may have considered using in their writing. At the end of the lesson he reminded the children of the intended learning outcome for the lesson. James then asked the children to exchange their work with a peer who carefully scrutinised the work for the use of connectives, which they were asked to highlight. Children were asked to work in pairs for the remainder of the lesson. They were challenged to communicate to their partner two positive comments about their partner's work and to consider one way in which the work could be enhanced.

Reflection

> Carefully consider the ways in which you could create a supportive ethos to facilitate peer assessment.
> What are the pitfalls of peer assessment and how could you avoid them?
> What are the benefits of peer assessment?

Professional development

During your placement seek permission to complete a short work scrutiny. Collect samples of children's work from a range of abilities and classes across the school. Focus on the feedback to the children by the teacher and consider the following.

> Is there any evidence that the children were aware of the success criteria?
> Do the teachers' comments relate to the success criteria?
> Are the teachers' comments positive?
> Do the teachers offer suggestions for further development to support the child's learning?
> Is there any evidence that the children have been provided with opportunities to act on feedback?
> Are there any examples of vague comments which the children may have found unhelpful?

A word of caution is needed. The above points demonstrate elements of effective practice. They are for you to consider and we strongly recommend that you do not make negative comments about the work of a qualified teacher.

Link to research

Pollard and Triggs (2000) carried out research into children's apprehensions in relation to teacher feedback on their work. The researchers found that as children became older they became increasingly apprehensive about the process of receiving feedback. Children in the early years and KS1 considered the feedback process to be a very positive experience. However, their confidence rapidly diminished and by the end of Year 6 only 13 per cent of children were comfortable with sharing their work with their teacher. It became apparent in the research that children were unable to identify the specific criteria through which teachers assessed their work, often assuming that the presentation and 'correctness' of the work would please the teacher.

Flutter and Rudduck (2004) found that children did not understand vague phrases which teachers used on children's work. Such comments included phrases such as *You must try harder.*

Black and Wiliam (1998a) found that formative assessment impacted positively on pupils' learning. The researchers argued that 'improved formative assessment helps the (so-called) low attainers more than the rest, and so reduces the spread of attainment whilst also raising it overall' (Black and Wiliam, 1998b: 4).

> How will the research impact on the way in which you offer feedback to children about their work?
> How will you ensure that your feedback to children about their work is meaningful and supportive?
> How will you ensure that children understand the criteria through which their work is being assessed?

Further reading

Clarke, S. (2001) *Unlocking Formative Assessment: Practical Strategies for Enhancing Pupils' Learning in the Primary Classroom.* London: Hodder and Stoughton.
This text provides a clear and comprehensive overview of formative assessment. It reflects on the advantages and pitfalls of formative assessment.

Glazzard, J., Chadwick, D., Webster, A. and Percival, J. (2010) *Assessment for Learning in the Early Years Foundation Stage.* London: Sage.
This text provides useful information on approaches for developing assessment for learning in the EYFS and on ways of involving parents, carers and children in the assessment process.

Useful websites

www.qcda.gov.uk/assessment
This site provides information about the statutory assessment requirements for primary schools.

www.nationalstrategies.standards.dcsf.gov.uk/primary/assessment/
This site provides information and guidance on teacher assessment at KS1 and KS2.

6

Team work

This chapter covers

In this chapter we emphasise the importance of collaborative working practices and the ways in which you can work towards achieving these. We identify the umbrella of experience and expertise both within and external to schools which contributes to children's holistic development.

Working with support staff

We use 'support staff' as a generic term to cover all practitioners who are responsible for supporting learning. Each of these professionals is a valuable human resource and should be deployed effectively to support children's cognitive, social and emotional development. Their skills and experience will be vast and varied. It is essential that you begin your placement with this acknowledgement in mind, engaging them in dialogue to ascertain their individual strengths, interests and roles.

Such professionals may be responsible for a range of professional duties which could include the following:

> specific targeted support for a child with special educational needs or a child with English as an additional language;
> specific support for groups of learners within the classroom (classroom assistants);
> targeted support for groups of learners following specific intervention programmes;

> part-time or full-time involvement with a class;
> higher level teaching assistants who supervise classes in the absence of a teacher;
> preparing resources and creating displays;
> supporting children with special educational needs in special units;
> cleaning staff and lunchtime supervisors;
> secretaries/administration staff;
> caretaker;
> staff who support extra-curricular activities. (adapted from Medwell, 2007)

It is essential that you understand and acknowledge that different people working in the school have a vital role to play in the efficient running of the school. Each member of staff is part of a very important team and should be treated with due respect. You should take time to introduce yourself to the wider team of professionals employed in the school. They may be willing to discuss their roles with you and if so, value and remember this information.

In working with additional adults it is likely that you will spend much of your time working with classroom assistants. Take time to engage them in discussions relating to their interests, strengths and roles in the class. Attempt to establish a relationship based on mutual respect. Initially this may involve a great deal of listening on your part but it will be time well spent. You will pick up valuable information which will support you throughout your placement. You need to identify the skills, knowledge and interests of your classroom assistant. This will enable you to deploy them effectively to support learning, behaviour and children's social and emotional needs.

Discuss with the class teacher and classroom assistant(s) the current systems of classroom organisation. The following prompts may support you.

> Ask them to identify the times during the week when they will be working with you in the classroom.
> What are their current responsibilities? Do they run groups or support individuals?
> Do they work with the same group or different groups?
> Are systems established to include classroom assistants in the planning and assessment process?
> Do classroom assistants support learners or do they have other classroom duties?
> How does the class teacher communicate intended learning outcomes to classroom assistants?

> Does the class teacher involve classroom assistants in identifying specific targets for groups of learners or individuals, including those with special educational needs?
> In what aspects of the curriculum do classroom assistants offer support?

The roles of classroom assistants are wide and will vary from school to school. However, they are increasingly involved in supporting learning and many have undertaken professional development to enhance their abilities to fulfil these roles. Whilst this section offers general advice on ways of working effectively with classroom assistants, a variety of practices will exist in different schools and even between classes in one school. You should therefore aim to adhere to the policies of the setting in which you are placed, whilst taking from here any advice that will support you and enhance your practice.

Existing classroom systems must not be changed during your placement. They will have been well considered and will have been selected with a purpose in mind. They will be understood by everyone, including the children, and you must ensure that you become familiar with them and adopt them early in your placement. You may not agree with specific systems, such as the ways in which support staff are deployed. You have a right to your views and opinions but it is very unwise to voice them and as a guest in the school you are required to follow policies and procedures, not change them.

Good communication with classroom assistants is essential. This should be professional and respectful. Ensure that you explicitly communicate intended learning outcomes where classroom assistants are specifically involved in supporting learning. You need to make the purposes of the activities clear and ensure that you have clearly explained how tasks should be structured. Involve classroom assistants in the assessment process. Ask them to make judgements about whether or not children have achieved the intended learning outcomes and involve them in discussions relating to learners' next steps. Classroom assistants should be invited to suggest children's next steps in learning whenever possible. They should also be encouraged to suggest possible tasks to address learners' next steps, thus involving them in the assessment–planning cycle. We have suggested the use of a simple and manageable format to enable classroom assistants to record children's achievements against the learning outcomes for the activity in Chapter 5.

Support assistants may work with you to support individuals or small groups of learners with special educational needs. You must both be familiar with the focused targets identified on individual education plans and will need to work in collaboration to identify and evidence children's achievements. In partnership with the class teacher, parents or carers, support assistant and child you will review children's progress against specified targets and together you will identify future targets to support learning. When planning for children with special educational needs support assistants will hold a wealth of knowledge and experience and may be able to support you very effectively in differentiating learning to meet their individual needs.

You will need to think carefully about how you deploy classroom assistants whilst you are working with the whole class. They should always have a role. You may consider deploying them as follows.

> Classroom assistants could carry out focused observations on specific children and note children's responses to learning.
> They could support individual learners with social, emotional and behaviour difficulties by helping them to focus during whole-class sessions.
> They could offer enhanced support to individuals by breaking down the learning, reiterating instructions, providing additional scaffolding to support learners' understanding, or by the use of additional modelling, demonstration or questioning to help children access the learning.
> They could be involved in enhancing the classroom environment through creating learning areas, displaying children's work and preparing resources.
> They could support individuals or groups of learners who are unable to access the learning, for example through the use of focused intervention programmes during whole-class sessions or linked learning which relates to the whole-class input but is suitably differentiated.
> They could support you in delivering the lesson.

Think carefully about how you deploy classroom assistants during the main part of the lesson. Consider the following.

> Will the classroom assistant support a group of learners?
> Will they support an individual learner within a group?
> Will they support an individual learner outside of a group?
> Will they be engaged in supporting a group of learners (or a whole class) by working collaboratively with you?
> Will they be engaged in the assessment process by standing back and observing a specific group of learners?

Consider the effective deployment of classroom assistants during the plenary. This may involve them leading 'mini-plenaries' with the groups they have been working with or may engage them in a whole-class plenary working alongside you.

The ways in which you will deploy classroom assistants will vary. What is of paramount importance is that they are consistently deployed effectively in the interests of the children. Effective communication is essential and enables your support staff to enhance and support your practices. Effective deployment of support staff will 'ensure that all learners make progress so that they fully achieve the challenging intended learning outcomes' (Ofsted, 2009: 29). Working in collaboration is the most effective way to maximise learners' progress and a focus on learner progress should enable you to achieve outstanding outcomes on your placement.

Effective ways of working with your mentor(s)

As you begin your placement it is essential that you start to establish good relationships with your mentor(s). In most contexts much of the support for your professional development will be gained through contact with your class teacher. In this section we refer to this professional as the 'class mentor'.

To support you effectively the class mentor will require a clear understanding of your strengths as a trainee teacher as well as the identification of areas for development. It is essential that you share your action plan with the class mentor if the class mentor is to fully support you and aid you in your professional development. The action plan must specify the targets that you intend to focus on for the duration of your placement, the strategies you intend to employ to address these and the success criteria against which your achievements will be measured. Your ITT provider should work with you to formulate this action plan. Initially you will need to discuss with the class mentor focused targets for your development. You must take responsibility for your own professional development. This will involve regular discussions about progress towards your targets with your class mentor and you will need to evidence your achievements throughout the placement. Your targets will be reviewed regularly and new areas for your professional development will be identified throughout the placement. We stress that you have a professional responsibility to be able to reflect honestly upon your own progress. In discussions with your class mentor you are therefore expected to take an active part in identifying your strengths and weaknesses, and you must take shared ownership of the steps you will take to address your targets. Passive trainees are rarely outstanding.

Take the time to become familiar with policies, systems and routines within the school and class and ensure that you work within these. Spend time observing and working alongside your class mentor and be willing and open to the opportunity to learn from more experienced colleagues. This will support you in understanding the ways in which policy and practice marry together.

Have the confidence to ask questions, especially during your initial visits to the school. You are not expected to know everything but you are expected to demonstrate a willingness to develop your understanding. Spend time observing how your class mentor uses a range of strategies for developing learners' confidence and self-esteem. There will be a range of verbal and non-verbal strategies. Facial expressions, a smile and good eye contact can convey as strong a response as words. Observe the ways in which your class mentor uses praise and reward systems to celebrate effort and achievement and note the ways in which the children respond to these. Identify the ways in which behavioural expectations are conveyed and how inappropriate behaviour is addressed. It is important that you identify the range of teaching strategies employed by the class mentor and that you understand the systems for classroom organisation, curricular organisation and classroom management. You should spend time during your initial visits developing a clear understanding of the context in which you will be working. Your ability to work within existing systems will support your learners to make a smooth transition between working with the class mentor and yourself. We suggest that you should consider innovative developments of your own. Many class mentors will welcome fresh ideas but you should ensure that any innovations are discussed and debated with the professionals that you are working with. Well-considered reflection relating to practices is usually welcomed.

Effective ways of working with colleagues across the school

During your placement take opportunities to work with colleagues across the school. Other colleagues undertake a range of roles and responsibilities and will have a wealth of experience and expertise to share with you. These will include:

> subject leaders;
> assessment leaders;
> departmental/Key Stage leaders;
> special needs coordinator/inclusion coordinator;
> safeguarding officer;
> health and safety officer;
> senior mentor (nominated person responsible for all ITT trainees in a school);

> head teacher;
> other classroom teachers;
> educational visits coordinator.

During the initial visits to the school identify the people undertaking the above roles. Identify opportunities to discuss and observe their work. It is your responsibility to pursue your own professional development across the life of the school. Take the opportunity to consider your own needs as identified on your action plan and meet with relevant colleagues across the school to address your training targets. Observe teachers working across the school and note differing teaching styles, approaches to classroom management and systems for classroom organisation. Seek opportunities to shadow key professionals within school to further develop your understanding of their work.

During your placement identify opportunities to work with colleagues across the school as they engage in CPD. Most schools will welcome your participation in whole-school training. There may also be additional opportunities for you to attend local authority training courses with teachers from your placement school. School-based colleagues access training in a range of ways including:

> school-based training, for example INSET days, staff meetings;
> school cluster meetings;
> local authority training;
> attendance at conferences.

You may have the opportunity to access some of the above training. It is unlikely that you will access all of it. However, during your placement teaching colleagues and other professionals in school may well undertake professional development. There could be planned opportunities for them to disseminate information gained from training to colleagues. Ensure that you actively seek to attend dissemination meetings or approach the identified colleague who may be more than willing to share the training with you.

Throughout your placement you should seek opportunities to enhance your own professional development. Outstanding trainees 'take full responsibility for their own professional development' (Ofsted, 2009: 36). It is vital that you set yourself challenging targets and take action to address these through pursuing your own professional development. Following this you need to implement and then review, analyse and reflect on your own work in collaboration with your colleagues, taking account of their feedback. According to Ofsted outstanding trainees 'show high quality self-evaluation with clear focus on learners and setting challenging targets for their own professional development – including, for example, future career progression with evidence of implementation and further review, and critical analysis and reflection, taking full account of feedback from trainers and other professionals they work with' (2009: 32). The approaches described in this section should help you to demonstrate this.

📁 **Case study**

Nelson was a trainee teacher undertaking his final teaching placement in a primary school with specialist resource-based provision for children with ASD. The policy of the local authority was that children placed in the autistic resource-based provision were capable of being partially or fully included in mainstream classes. Nelson was working in the mixed EYFS/Year 1 class.

A new entrant to the resource-based provision (Owen) was being supported by practitioners in the resource-base in preparation for his partial inclusion in Nelson's class. Nelson identified this as an opportunity to further his own professional development. Through discussion with the class mentor and the professionals in the resource base Nelson was offered the opportunity to work in the base during his professional development time. This presented Nelson with the experience of observing Owen within the base. During these periods of observation Nelson gleaned the following information:

> Owen's capacity for social interaction;
> information about Owen's language and communication needs;
> information about Owen's dispositions and attitudes towards learning;
> effective strategies for supporting Owen's needs.

Nelson noted the strategies which effectively supported Owen. He subsequently worked in collaboration with the professionals from both the resource base and mainstream class as they worked together to share information and plan a smooth transition between settings to effectively support Owen. Nelson was able to take a leading role in the discussions and with support he was able to use the strategies he had previously observed as well as the knowledge he had acquired to effectively support Owen's transition to the mainstream class.

Reflection

> Consider ways in which you can identify opportunities in your placement school to enhance your own professional development through first-hand experiences.
> How did collaborative working support Nelson in developing his own understanding of ASD and effective transition?
> How might this opportunity shape Nelson's own professional identity?

Effective ways of working with external agencies

Current educational policy agenda emphasises the importance of multi-agency working practices to achieve the best outcomes for all learners. Many of your school-based colleagues will work in partnership with other professionals outside school to support individual learners with specific needs as well as to support learning within the school. These could include:

> medical professionals;
> educational psychologists;
> behaviour support workers;
> child and mental health professionals;
> learning support professionals to support children with special educational needs or language and communication needs;
> emergency services;
> social services professionals.

This is not an exhaustive list and there will be other professionals working in partnership with the school. You should seek opportunities to research the roles and responsibilities of the wider professional workforce and to identify those who work in collaboration with your school, its learners and families. We would suggest that you begin by discussing this with your class mentor, who will be best placed to direct you to other specialised professionals working within the school, for example the special educational needs coordinator/inclusion coordinator and safeguarding officer. In turn these school-based colleagues will be able to identify the external agencies with which they work and further explain the roles and responsibilities of these professionals. Communicate your interest in developing a deeper understanding of the roles of people working for external agencies. School-based colleagues may be happy to identify opportunities for you to meet with external professionals who may be visiting the school during your placement. Opportunities to observe such professionals at work may arise. It should be noted that for you this will be a process of observation rather than participation. The following are examples of the ways in which you may observe visiting professionals from external agencies:

> annual review meetings for children with statements of special educational needs;
> speech therapists working with specific children or the class teacher;

> educational psychologists undertaking assessments of specific children;
> behaviour support workers or other specialist colleagues supporting children with specific educational needs.

You should note ways in which external professionals work in partnership with your school-based colleagues to support individual learners. Outstanding trainees 'demonstrate an understanding of the range of professionals that contribute to learners' overall development and their place in the "bigger picture" – well informed discussion about individual/groups of learners and particular needs' (Ofsted, 2009: 34).

Payne argues that 'power struggles about objectives, roles and responsibilities are major impediments to collaboration' (2000: 26). Effective multi-agency working is reliant upon a clear understanding of different roles and responsibilities, systems, policies and effective communication and trust. Different professionals need to demonstrate a willingness to work in collaboration and be open-minded to different perspectives.

Effective ways of working with parents and carers

Working effectively in collaboration with parents and carers is a key professional skill and one that you are required to demonstrate for the award of QTS. Communicating and developing effective partnerships with parents is embedded within the professional standards for trainee teachers. The development of effective partnerships with parents and carers impacts positively on outcomes for learners and is a key strand of the current educational policy agenda.

At the beginning of your placement you must establish positive relationships with parents and carers. Initially you must introduce yourself. Additionally good eye contact, a smile and a simple acknowledgement of their presence will aid you in beginning the process of establishing effective relationships with them. Find out about the policies relating to parent partnership. The school may operate an open-door policy and this will facilitate the process of developing good working relationships with parents and carers. If you are working in the EYFS the school may have already begun to develop relationships with parents through home–school visits prior to children's entry into full-time education. If you have the opportunity to accompany professionals on such visits you should capitalise on this. Be aware that in some schools there is more of a closed-door policy in relation to working with parents. It is important that you familiarise yourself with the policies of the school in which you are placed and adhere to these.

Schools often communicate with parents and carers and develop partnerships in a range of ways including:

> newsletters, which provide information about curriculum coverage and school information;
> school website;
> virtual learning environment;
> home–school diaries which facilitate communication between school and home, and home and school;
> parent workshops;
> parent consultation meetings;
> parent notice boards;
> involving parents in school visits;
> sharing targets with parents and carers;
> homework;
> parents working within classrooms;
> systems for sharing achievements between school and home, and home and school;
> systems for working with parents as partners in learning for children with special educational needs.

This is not an exhaustive list and you should research the ways in which your particular school addresses this very important working partnership. Some schools may be developing practices which focus specifically on the engagement of fathers in working in partnership with the school. You must familiarise yourself with the school policy on parent partnership and the home–school agreement. Identify with your class mentor the ways in which you can support and promote the implementation of the parent partnership policies. Before inviting parents or carers to support you as a practitioner you must ensure that you adhere to the school policies on safeguarding and promoting the welfare of children.

Working in partnership with parents and carers should be positive, productive and beneficial to learners. Unfortunately there may be occasions when you will encounter challenging situations. As a trainee teacher you are advised to consult with your mentor in relation to such issues. There may be opportunities for you to work alongside your mentor as these more challenging situations are addressed. It is unadvisable to face such challenges without the support of well-informed and experienced practitioners.

Take advantage of all opportunities offered to you to communicate with and report to parents and carers. This could involve supporting your class mentor in a parent consultation meeting.

📁 **Case study**

Mia was a trainee teacher undertaking a second teaching placement. One morning she was approached by an aggressive parent, who had a clear expectation that Mia should deal with her concerns. The parent was unhappy about the way in which Mia had dealt with her child on the previous day. Mia was unable to address the problem immediately but reassured the parent that she would be available to discuss the problem at the end of the day. This provided Mia with valuable thinking time and the opportunity to seek professional advice from more experienced colleagues. The parent returned at the end of the day to discuss the problem with both Mia and the class mentor. The class mentor allowed Mia to lead the meeting but was available for support. Mia started the meeting by thanking the parent for attending and she asked the parent to sit down. Mia provided the parent with an opportunity to express her concerns. Whilst the parent talked, Mia made notes, whilst listening carefully to the parent's concerns. She also maintained eye contact with the parent. As the meeting progressed the parent noticeably became calm. Mia responded to the points raised by the parent and she explained why she had dealt with the child in a specific way. The parent was satisfied with the outcomes of the meeting.

Reflection

> Why was it important for Mia to delay the meeting?
> How did Mia ensure that the parent felt comfortable at the start of the meeting?
> How did Mia demonstrate to the parent that her concerns were taken seriously?
> How did Mia protect herself in the meeting?
> What other complaints might parents make and how might you address these?

Working with the child as a partner in learning

The United Nations *Convention on the Rights of the Child* stipulates that:

State Parties shall assure to the child who is capable of forming his/her own views the right to express those views freely in all matters affecting the child, the views of the child being given due weight in accordance with the age and maturity of the child. (1990: Article 12)

The importance of listening to and acting upon children's voices in education is a fundamental principle of the current policy agenda. A pre-requisite of working effectively with children is to develop and establish strong relationships which are built on mutual respect and trust.

Children must be consulted and involved as partners in their own learning and development. This entitlement may be addressed through some of the following ways.

> Involve children in the planning of their own learning by engaging them in expressing their own interests and creating opportunities to enable them to follow their own lines of enquiry.
> Involving children in the assessment process is crucial and has been dis-cussed in Chapter 5 – children set their own targets and review their own progress.
> Involve children in evaluating your teaching.
> Children with special educational needs should be involved in review pro-cesses and the identification of new targets in line with the *Special Educational Needs Code of Practice* (DfES, 2001).
> Provide children with opportunities to influence policies and practices at both school and class level through the creation of school and class councils.
> Facilitate opportunities for children to share their out-of-school experiences with their peers, for example through the use of a community board or circle time.
> A sealed postbox can provide an opportunity to post confidential messages to practitioners. These must be checked on a daily basis. Messages can be anonymous but children requiring direct support would need to identify themselves on the note to ensure that their concerns can be addressed.

In all schools there will be initiatives to support children's participation in education. You may have some innovative ideas of your own which would be welcomed by your school. It is important that you discuss these before imple-menting them as they must adhere to school policies and practices.

Woods (1976) and Meighan (1977) both emphasised the value of consulting children on their views in relation to teaching and learning. Therefore the notion of child voice in education is not new. Rudduck et al. (1996) introduced the notion of using child voice as a contributing factor to school improve-ment. Rudduck (2006) introduced the concept of two strands associated with child voice – *consultation* and *participation*. Consultation relates to children's involvement in the development of policies, initiatives, teaching and learning. Participation engages children through the formation of committees, working parties and groups to solve problems. Within a model of participation children are part of decision-making processes and participate in managing their own learning. Sammons et al. (1995) found a positive correlation between increased self-esteem and the development of pupil voice. Futurelab (2006) emphasised the need for schools to avoid a tokenistic commitment to learner voice and that the quality of the level of learner engagement needs to be further addressed.

Professional development

Identify opportunities to visit other schools to research the differing ways in which partnerships with parents and carers have been developed. Discuss your research with colleagues within your own placement school. This will support you in understanding the ways in which effective systems adopted by one school could be ineffective in another. Equally this may afford you the opportunity of sharing good practice which could be adopted by your own school.

Link to research

Crozier (1997) found that working-class parents are less likely than middle-class parents to support children's academic development. Crozier and Davies (2006) found that some ethnic groups living in England, particularly Bangladeshi and Pakistani, lacked the knowledge of how to support their children at home. Lareau (2000) found that both working- and middle-class parents were willing to support their children at home but the middle-class parents deployed more strategies to help their children's academic development whilst working-class parents were often intimidated by teachers. This research suggests that generally parents have a desire to support their children's academic development but that some groups are more capable of doing so than others. The research has implications for the ways in which teachers engage parents in their child's learning. Schools may therefore need to consider how they communicate learning needs to parents of different ethnic groups and how these parents can support their child's learning. Specific workshops to help parents understand what their child is learning in school and how this learning is supported may serve as useful strategies to help parents support their children. Adult education programmes may have a positive impact on children's learning.

Further reading

Alexander, R. (2010) 'Children's voices', in R. Alexander (ed.), *Children, their World, their Education: Final Report and Recommendations of the Cambridge Primary Review*. Abingdon, Oxon: Routledge. pp. 17–48.
This text is a comprehensive independent review of primary education. It focuses on key aspects of primary education and draws together findings from an extensive research base.

Barron, I., Holmes, R., MacLure, M. and Runswick-Cole, K. (2010) 'Primary schools and other agencies', in R. Alexander (ed.), *The Cambridge Primary Review: Research Surveys*. London: Routledge. pp. 97–135.
This chapter provides a historical overview of the relationship between education and external agencies which support vulnerable learners.

Robinson, C. and Fielding, M. (2010) 'Children and their primary schools: pupils' voices', in R. Alexander (ed.), *The Cambridge Primary Review: Research Surveys*. Abingdon, Oxon: Routledge.
This chapter provides a comprehensive summary of children's views on their primary education. The chapter focuses on children's views of learning, teaching, the curriculum and assessment.

Whalley, M. (2007) *Involving Parents in their Children's Learning*, 2nd edn. London: Sage.
This text illustrates the pioneering work of the Pen Green Centre for children and families. It exemplifies effective parent partnerships and explains how parents can support children. The book provides strategies for facilitating the involvement of fathers and male carers.

Useful websites

www.education.gov.uk/aboutdfe/policiesandprocedures/ppm/b00138/project-management/project-start-up/building-your-team
This website provides you with valuable information about building your team. This will help you to understand how effective teams operate.

www.education.gov.uk/schools/pupilsupport/parents
This website provides comprehensive guidance on parental partnership. It includes specific information on parental responsibility and Parent Teacher Associations.

www.teachernet.gov.uk/wholeschool/supportstaff/
This website provides information on working with other adults.

7

Classroom management

This chapter covers

In this chapter we consider strategies for managing the learning environment and children's behaviour. We specifically address ways in which you might encourage children to talk through conflicts and strategies for managing low level and more challenging behaviour. In the research focus the underpinning theories of behaviour management are also explored.

Classroom management often causes trainee teachers a great deal of anxiety. During the early stages of your training you may have concerns about whether you will be able to effectively manage children's behaviour. However, as you gain experience teaching classes your confidence will gradually develop. Confident trainees have a good *teacher presence*. Their learners essentially see them as teachers rather than as a friend or a helper. Consequently they are able to command respect. However, respect should be mutual and you need to convey to your learners that you respect them and value them as individuals before you can expect them to respect you. To demonstrate that you respect your learners it is important that you:

> listen to what they have to say;
> show an interest in them as individuals, for example in their likes and dislikes at school and at home;
> model appropriate behaviours when dealing with conflict;

> apply fair, clear and consistent sanctions, which should be graduated to take into account the severity of the incident;
> deal with an incident and then move forward with no further reference to it;
> use positive praise when the child is demonstrating desired behaviours.

Managing conflict

It is important that conflicts are managed appropriately and effectively. It is also important that conflicts are managed in private. No child should ever be humiliated. Managing a conflict should begin by giving the child a voice. The aim is to ascertain the reasons for the conflict. Additionally you must seek to ensure that the child fully understands why the behaviour was inappropriate. Young children in particular do not always understand the difference between right and wrong and sometimes have limited strategies for dealing with events that they find upsetting. It is the role of the adult to empower children by introducing them to a range of strategies and support systems to enable them to deal with challenging situations. It is essential that you keep an open mind during any discussions with the child. Children can deflect blame away from themselves by transferring it to others. Ensure that you are clear about events before taking any action.

As a trainee teacher you need to be familiar with the behaviour policy of the school in which you are working. This should make it clear that designated members of staff will be able to support you in managing children's behaviour. The policy should also outline whole-school systems for managing challenging behaviour as well as rewarding positive attitudes towards behaviour and work. You may have the opportunity to develop your own systems for rewards and sanctions. You should discuss these with your mentor prior to their implementation.

Children should be involved in the development of classroom systems which address challenging behaviour and rewards. You should provide children with an opportunity to be involved in the development of rules and sanctions. This will give them ownership and a clearer understanding of the expectations of adults and peers. Effective teachers negotiate behaviour contracts with their learners. Consistency on your part is essential and central to managing challenging behaviours and rewarding children. Children usually respond to clear expectations but will also quickly identify a teacher who is inconsistent in applying them.

Most teachers will have adopted whole-school policies relating to sanctions and rewards but will have adapted these to meet the needs of the children in their class. Effective systems in a class of Year 6 children could be totally inappropriate for a class of Year 1 children. If children have a clear understanding of class sanctions and rewards they should be supported to articulate the way in which their behaviour will be addressed. If they are unable to do this then a clear explanation will be needed.

When addressing a negative incident it is essential that this is concluded. All children need an opportunity to move forward from such a situation. There is seldom a justifiable reason to inform parents and carers of the incident as this could result in a child receiving a second sanction for the same incident. However, on occasions where children repeatedly display the same inappropriate behaviours it is important to discuss these with parents or carers. In these situations it would be evident that the sanctions employed were ineffective and there would be a need to develop a behaviour contract or plan in consultation with the child, parents and carers, and the school. Such contracts should be supportive of the child.

Children with extremely challenging behaviour may receive support from outside agencies. Some may have a statement of special educational needs. Current educational policy agenda emphasises the importance of effective multi-agency collaboration. During your placement you may have an opportunity to shadow a colleague in school as they work with outside agencies to support a child. This experience would support you in identifying, understanding and implementing effective strategies to address challenging behaviours.

Addressing the behaviour rather than the child

When you manage conflict it is essential to ensure that the child's self-esteem is always preserved. Children need to know that it is the behaviour that is undesirable rather than themselves. This can be addressed in the following ways.

> Avoid the use of the word 'you': Replace *I don't like the way you have pushed other children* with *I wonder how children feel when they are pushed*?
> Discuss the behaviour without directly attaching it to the child.
> Explain why the behaviour is inappropriate rather than why they have behaved inappropriately.
> Focus on the desired behaviour by asking them to consider alternative ways of dealing with such a conflict.
> Speak in the third person rather than the second person.

Ultimately children need to be supported to take responsibility for their own actions. You may consider offering children short opportunities for quiet reflection. For all children it is essential to ascertain that they understand why their actions or behaviours were inappropriate and some children may need to be supported in developing and communicating this understanding. Give children an opportunity to articulate why their behaviour was inappropriate and provide them with the means to consider how they wish to resolve the issue.

Making expectations clear

When you need the attention of a group or whole class of children it is important that the children are clear about your expectations. An example of this is to say *I want you to look at me* rather than *Are we ready?* The former transmits a clear expectation; the latter can imply that the children have a choice. Avoid asking questions; give direct instructions. Other examples include the following.

> *I want you to stop talking please* rather than *Please can we stop taking now?*
> *I want you to listen please* rather than *Please will you listen to me?*
> *Stop playing with Jemma's hair please* as opposed to *Please can you stop playing with Jemma's hair?*

Clear instructions usually result in more immediate responses from children. Positive behaviour strategies are to be celebrated but it is important to realise that they do not work for all children. Some children or groups of children respond more positively to a clear, concise instruction. Consider avoiding the word 'please' at the beginning of an instruction. This word should not be omitted as it models respectful communication with others. Stating a command followed by the word 'please' is clear, concise and polite, and demonstrates respect for the listeners.

It is important to ensure that all children are listening before you begin talking to them. If only a few children are listening whilst others continue their conversations, you are conveying to them that this is acceptable. In turn ensure that you also listen carefully and do not interrupt children when they are speaking to the group or class. Some alternative and useful strategies for gaining children's attention are listed as follows.

> Use non-verbal strategies, such as a picture which communicates the need to stop talking or working, to gain their attention.
> Use a short and familiar piece of music, for example to signal the end of a session and the need to tidy away, or the need to assemble in a specific place.

> Use a count down clock, for example on the interactive whiteboard.
> Use a noise meter to control the level of noise within the classroom.
> Use a sequence of physical actions which children can join in with.
> Use clapping rhythms which children can join in with, although do not over-use this strategy and keep any chosen rhythm short.
> Use 'empty hands'.
> Use proximal praise: praise children who are listening and adhering to expectations in order to encourage those who need further support to achieve expectations.
> Use a known chant, for example 1, 2, 3 look at me!

Your body language is also a strong means of communicating your expectations to the children. Some children respond effectively to simple facial expressions, for example:

> raised eyebrows;
> shaking your head from side to side;
> holding a glance;
> a frown;
> a smile.

Non-verbal communication is a valuable tool in conveying expectations to children. It has the advantage of minimising the disruption to the flow of a lesson.

In this section we have suggested a range of strategies for gaining the attention of children as well as dealing with low level disruption. You may also like to consider strategies of your own. Bear in mind that even minor disruptions should be dealt with immediately. If they are allowed to run and build they can have a very negative impact on teaching and learning for all children. With a new class time spent conveying your expectations is time well spent and you and the children will benefit from this in the long term, especially when your expectations may differ from those of the class teacher.

It is important to reflect on the reasons for inappropriate responses from children. These could include:

> lack of challenge in the lesson;
> too much challenge;
> lack of presence on the part of the teacher;
> lack of clarity in terms of expectations for behaviour and/or work;

> lack of consistency and routines;
> external factors which negatively impact on the social skills of the children (hunger, thirst, difficulties at home) – a key professional standard is to understand the factors which impact on learning and development;
> children feeling unwell;
> lack of opportunities for physical activity;
> lack of motivation due to inappropriate teaching styles.

Consider using visual, auditory and kinaesthetic strategies within lessons. Children do not always need to be seated at a table. Think carefully about opportunities for fostering motivation through developing learning in the outdoors. Try to provide children with quality first-hand experiences and opportunities for enquiry-based learning.

This is not an exhaustive list. It is important to be aware of children who find it challenging to work together. These children may need to be separated in order to avoid disruption to themselves and others and to maximise opportunities for learning and participation.

Sanctions

The use of sanctions should be seen as a positive strategy to support a child in understanding the ways in which their actions or behaviours affect others. These will usually only be applied after the behavioural expectation has already been explained. Sanctions provide an opportunity to remove a child calmly from a situation they find challenging and provide them with a short period of time to quietly reflect on their own behaviour and reasons for it. The use of a 'time-out' strategy can be effective if the strategy is applied in the following way.

> Calmly remove a child from the conflict.
> Provide the child with a private space for quiet reflection, ensuring that the child is supervised by an adult.
> After a short period of time to reflect, approach the child in an unthreatening manner.
> Position yourself at the level of the child, ensuring that your facial expressions and body language are non-confrontational.
> Ask the child if they understand why you both need to talk.
> Give the child a voice by providing them with an opportunity to express their views and offer explanations for their own behaviour.
> Ask the child to consider the impact of their behaviour on others and seek a response from the child.

> Discuss whole-school sanctions with the child and how these will be applied in the current situation; depending on the gravity of the incident no further action may be needed.
> Ask the child to articulate why the behaviour was inappropriate and their understanding of the consequences of their actions.
> Ask the child if there is any further action they wish to take (for example offer an apology to another child).
> Once the incident has been addressed it should not be mentioned again; children should be able to start again with a clean slate.

You should ensure that sanctions are applied to situations promptly. Young children in particular may find it difficult to relate an action to a sanction when the two are separated by a long period of time.

Dealing with persistent misbehaviour

Children who display persistent misbehaviour may need a behaviour plan to support them. Such a plan should state clear SMART targets for the child to work towards:

Specific

Measurable

Achievable

Realistic

Timed

When applying sanctions it is important to refer back to these targets and remind children of the goals which they are aiming to achieve. It is also essential that children's successes are acknowledged and celebrated. Children need to be involved in setting their own targets and reviewing their progress towards these.

Teaching children to talk through conflict

Sylva et al. emphasise the importance of supporting children in talking through and rationalising conflicts:

In settings that were less effective ... our observations showed that there was often no follow-up on children's misbehaviour and, on many occasions, children were 'distracted' or simply told to stop. (2004: 07)

Facilitate opportunities for children to discuss confrontations with one another. The role of the adult is to support such interactions, not to dominate them. Suggest that all children involved in a dispute should be offered an opportunity to speak to the group. As each child speaks it is important that the others listen. Children need to be supported to consider:

> why the incident happened;
> the effect(s) of any undesirable behaviours on others;
> how it could have been dealt with differently;
> an acknowledgement of any wrong doing by a child or children;
> ways in which the conflict might be resolved.

This strategy will enable children to begin to acknowledge the perspectives of others and the effects of their actions on people's feelings. Children should be encouraged to reflect on the views, feelings and needs of others and to understand that these should be treated with respect.

The link between children's behaviour and classroom organisation

Effective classroom organisation helps to minimise disruptions caused by inappropriate behaviours. Poor organisation usually results in:

> children queuing to see the teacher;
> children off task because too many need help at the same time;
> increased noise levels;
> children becoming disruptive;
> inadequate learning;
> teachers 'servicing' children rather than teaching a focused group.

In developing effective systems of classroom organisation you may find it helpful to plan activities using a traffic light system.

> **Red activities**: these are 'teacher intensive' tasks; the learners cannot progress without adult input; these tasks are usually adult-led teacher-guided activities.
> **Amber activities**: these are less teacher intensive activities in which some occasional support is required from adults in order to help learners make progress.

> **Green activities**: these are independent activities which consolidate prior learning; children can progress in their learning with minimal supervision as they have already been introduced to the key concepts, skills or aspects of knowledge; these learners are still making progress because they are independently applying the knowledge, skills and concepts which they have already been taught.

Ideally it is more effective if only one 'red' activity is operational so that the teacher can focus on giving high quality guided teaching to a specific group of learners. If you have support staff working with you it will be possible to organise more of these activities. This model of organisation will minimise queuing, and teacher stress, and provide valuable opportunities for children to learn to work independently.

Activity

You are teaching a group of Reception children and the focus of the session is to introduce the children to the phoneme *igh*. This group is working to national expectations but there are both lower and higher attaining children within the cohort. The teacher is following the *Letters and Sounds* scheme (DfES, 2006). How could the teacher teach this focused group activity whilst ensuring that the others are actively and purposefully engaged without the support of an adult.

Developing positive classroom management strategies

Effective behaviour management should always preserve children's self-esteem. Aim to focus on positive behaviour. Do not simply accept good behaviour; ensure that you acknowledge it. Children who always behave often get overlooked and explicitly celebrating positive behaviour enables such children to exemplify expectations and be role models. Additionally it is important to celebrate good behaviour amongst all children. For children with social, emotional and behavioural difficulties this will be a powerful way of raising their self-esteem.

A variety of strategies can be employed to facilitate this and might include:

> individual rewards, for example stickers, certificates, treats;
> group rewards, for example team points;
> verbal praise;

> systems for accumulating praise, leading to a reward;
> systems for facilitating peer–peer support such as *Circle of Friends*; within this model children acknowledge one another's positive attributes.

Case study

In a Year 1 classroom the children are encouraged to engage in a short circle time each day. The focus is for them to consider the different ways in which members of the class have been kind. Adults also model the different ways in which kindness can be shown. Children must nominate a peer and not themselves and explain the ways in which kindness has been demonstrated. Each day one act of kindness is selected by the group. This is subsequently written on a kindness leaf and added to the kindness tree. As the children further develop their understanding of kindness they are encouraged to access the kindness leaves independently and write their own messages to their peers. Practitioners also contribute to this process.

Reflection

> How could this strategy benefit a child with social, emotional and behavioural difficulties?
> Consider other systems for acknowledging positive behaviour. Share these with your peers.

Case study

Harry is 9 years old and has a recent statement for special educational needs relating to behaviour, emotional and social development. The school is currently working towards including him within a mainstream class. He is supported by a teaching assistant for the majority of the time on an individual basis. The Behaviour Support Agency in the local authority advises the school on strategies to support Harry.

When Harry initially arrived at the school he considered himself to be 'bad'. He was unable to identify incidents of appropriate behaviour which did exist but were overshadowed in his mind by his memories of inappropriate behaviours. The staff in school worked with Harry to identify positive aspects of his behaviour. However, this was not particularly successful. Harry continued to see himself as 'bad'.

To address this, the school implemented a simple reward system. The day was divided into five sessions which included four teaching sessions and lunch time. All appropriate behaviours in each session were rewarded with a star which was placed on a chart. At the end of each session Harry was encouraged to evaluate his behaviour. Lots of stars were an indication of his successes. When he focused on a bad session he was assured that the session was now in the past and that he had an opportunity to start again in the subsequent session.

After several weeks Harry was asked to summarise his behaviour throughout a whole day. When Harry insisted he had had a bad day he was referred back to the chart which provided a visual record of his behaviour during the day. Harry continued to insist that even one bad session made it a bad day. With support from the teacher Harry was asked to evaluate each session throughout the day. Harry was then encouraged to identify the number of 'good' and 'bad' sessions and to realise that on some days there were more positives than negatives. This was celebrated. Harry quickly developed the ability to identify days as successful or unsuccessful by comparing the number of positive and negative sessions in terms of his behaviour.

Reflection

> How did the school support Harry to understand that one session of inappropriate behaviour did not result in the whole day being viewed in a negative light?
> Why do you think that Harry initially focused on his negative behaviours?
> Children with behavioural difficulties frequently view themselves negatively. Consider other strategies to build the self-esteem of these children. Discuss this with a peer or colleagues in school.
> Consider the other children and their thoughts and feelings in relation to Harry misbehaving and getting stickers. How might you address these?

Case study

Jameelia started full-time education in an early years setting at the age of 5. She lived with her parents and was the youngest of three children. Her siblings were both in their twenties. On entry to school she was socially and emotionally very immature. She had had little contact with other children and had spent much of her time with adults. Jameelia had developed few skills to express her emotions appropriately. Adults and children were pushed, hit and spat at when they did not meet her expectations.

(Continued)

(Continued)

The lead practitioner in the setting met with Jameelia's parents to discuss the difficulties she was facing. A behaviour plan was drawn up by the practitioner and parents. Jameelia was not involved in formulating targets because in previous interactions with adults she showed little understanding of the inappropriateness of her behaviour. The plan focused on ignoring specific behaviours but targeting those which were causing most distress to other children. Adults working closely with Jameelia ensured that she was praised for positive behaviours relating to her targets. Positive behaviour was rewarded through a simple chart showing pictures of each adult in the class. Each time Jameelia responded appropriately to other children or adults the behaviour was praised by the observing practitioner who placed a smiley face on their picture above the chart. At the end of each session Jameelia was asked to review her behaviour by referring to the chart. This provided a visual record of the number of times different adults had acknowledged her good behaviour.

Reflection

> The current educational policy agenda and the Code of Practice for special educational needs (DfES, 2001) advocates the importance of the voice of the child in decision-making processes. Why do you think that on this occasion Jameelia was not involved in this process?
> How could Jameelia have been consulted about her targets?

Finding your own strategies

This chapter has offered a range of ideas to support you in developing effective classroom management. Most teachers rely on a small bank of strategies which work for them. As you begin to develop your own professional identity you will implement, discard and adapt many systems as you work towards identifying those that you wish to adopt. The strategies that you use need to be shared with the children and you must convey a clear expectation that children will respond immediately to them.

You can develop your knowledge of behaviour management strategies through:

> observing experienced teachers;
> discussions with your ITT tutors;
> lectures;

> personal research;
> participating in educational forums.

You need to develop your own strategies which work for you. You are not a clone of any other professional. You are unique and what works for others may not work for you. From time to time even the most experienced teachers may be challenged by the behaviours and/or actions of some children. These instances provide valuable opportunities for you to reflect on your own practice. Children are unique and a well-tested strategy which has worked for several children may be ineffective with another child. It is crucial that you do not view such challenges as a failure on your part. You can seek support from more experienced teachers and develop further strategies to address the problem. Effective teachers develop strategies for managing children's challenging behaviour in consultation with pupils and parents. The following points should be considered in such situations.

> Consult with parents to determine whether there are any external factors which may be impacting negatively on the child's behaviour.
> Talk to the child to determine the reasons for their behaviour.
> Observe the triggers which result in behaviour problems and remove these if possible.
> Agree strategies for rewards and sanctions with the child.
> Agree targets with the child and in consultation with the child and parent(s) agree a behaviour contract.
> Consider whether the child will confide in or respond better to another known adult.
> Do not label a child as 'naughty'.
> Share successes with children.
> Ensure that children do understand why their behaviours or actions are inappropriate.

 Professional development

The National Strategies launched the Inclusion Development Programme in 2008. An e-learning course has recently been produced to address strategies for supporting children with behavioural, emotional and social difficulties. The materials can be found through accessing the following web link: nationalstrategies.standards.dcsf.gov.uk/search/inclusion/results/nav:46335?page=1

Work through the modules in this package to develop your understanding further.

Link to research

Hayes produces categories of children's 'silly' behaviour. These include:

> uncontrolled: shouting out an answer without permission;
> arrogant: being 'clever';
> distractive: doing something 'daring' to show off;
> detached: working slowly deliberately;
> insolent: asking pointless questions;
> deceptive: pretending that they do not understand. (2004: 270–72)

Hayes also produces a useful overview of the consequences of boredom in terms of how this often leads to a variety of off-task behaviours. He provides practical strategies for managing 'silly' behaviours. This work encourages teachers to reflect on the extent to which their own pedagogical approaches might be responsible for a range of undesirable behaviours in the classroom.

Further reading

Cowley, S. (2010) *Getting the Buggers to Behave*, 4th edn. London: Continuum.
This book is practical and accessible and provides readers with a range of practical strategies for managing children's behaviour.

Rogers, B. and McPherson, E. (2008) *Behaviour Management with Young Children: Crucial First Steps with Children 3–7 Years.* London: Sage.
The book focuses on behaviour management in the early years in a practical and accessible way. It covers aspects such as behaviour recovery practice, challenging behaviour and positive discipline.

Dukes, C. and Smith, M. (2009) *Building Better Behaviour in the Early Years*. London: Sage.
The book focuses on how to create a positive atmosphere, enabling environments, a team-based approach, and observing and assessing behaviour.

Useful websites

www.suecowley.co.uk/
This site includes handouts on rewards and sanctions.

www.teachernet.gov.uk/wholeschool/behaviour/
This site provides useful guidance on supporting children with social, emotional and behavioural difficulties, whole-school behaviour policies and bullying.

8

Pursuing your own
professional development

This chapter covers

According to Ofsted outstanding trainees 'take full responsibility for their own professional development' (2009: 36). This chapter examines ways in which you can take ownership of your own professional development to enable you to address your specific training targets. During your placements you will be expected to take responsibility for identifying and meeting your developing professional needs. This is a key professional standard. You should be able to reflect on your own practice and identify short-, medium- and long-term targets to support your professional development. Your professional targets are personal to you. Consequently this means that your training experience should also be shaped to meet your own needs. School-based mentors have a partial responsibility to provide training which addresses your individual needs. The onus for providing an individualised programme of training does not solely rest with your school-based trainers. You have a responsibility to identify emerging targets and you will be expected to be proactive in addressing these throughout your professional training. This chapter suggests strategies that should help you to address your emerging professional needs.

Becoming part of a learning community

As you progress through your ITT you will realise that good teachers are always learning. Teaching is a profession and to be successful and remain challenged you will need to continually identify new targets to focus on throughout your career. By the end of your professional training you will have a great deal more that you need to learn, even if you have been judged to be outstanding. Outstanding teachers continually challenge themselves academically and professionally to help them further develop their practice.

During your placements you will need to demonstrate that you are able to:

> identify new challenges/targets for yourself;
> take appropriate action to address these targets;
> reflect on the success of the actions taken.

Outstanding trainees view themselves as learners. The process of learning how to be an effective teacher will continue long after your professional training has ended. Education does not stand still. It continually evolves and you will need to ensure that your practice reflects current ideas and initiatives as you progress throughout your career. Seeing yourself as a 'learning professional' in this way is something you can embrace from your first teaching placement.

During post-lesson feedback sessions and reviews of progress with your professional mentors you will be expected to demonstrate that you are able to reflect on your own practice and identify your own emerging targets. Your mentor(s) will be able to suggest some ways in which you can address your targets. However, you can take ownership of your own targets through developing your own strategies for addressing your emerging professional needs. You will be able to identify some key targets that you want to focus on prior to the start of your placement. These might be longer-term targets. However, some targets will only become apparent during your placement. At the end of each week of teaching you should identify key targets that you want to focus on during the next week. These are medium-term targets and should be specific and measurable. Some targets might be short term and might need to be addressed in the next lesson. The key point is that you should be able to articulate your own strengths and identify areas for your own development. Outstanding trainees do not need to be informed about their targets. They are able to reflect on their own practice and identify their own areas for development. They are subsequently able to plan appropriate action to address their development needs. This process places an onus on you to be proactive and to take charge of your own professional development.

Reflecting on your own practice and identifying targets

The ability to reflect on your own strengths and areas for development is fundamental to being successful. At the end of each lesson you should engage in a process of reflection. You will need to identify what aspects were successful and what aspects needed to be improved, with a strong focus on the quality of pupils' learning. However, the process of reflection should also be carried out at the end of a day, a week, halfway through your placement and at the end of the placement. This process should enable you to identify your strengths and your emerging professional development needs.

Reflection should take place individually and collaboratively with school-based colleagues and provider link tutors. You will need to demonstrate that you can articulate your strengths and emerging needs; reflection can take place through oral interchanges, as well as through written commentaries on your own practice.

Prior to the start of your placement you should identify key targets that you need to address throughout your placement. These may have emerged from a previous placement. The identification of targets for the placement should be done in consultation with your ITT provider and school-based mentors. This process will enable you to draw up a placement action plan or individual training plan. This document is the starting point for shaping the training experience around your individual needs. Throughout your placement you should refer back to your training plan/action plan to monitor your progress towards your initial targets. The document can be used to set new targets on a week-by-week basis. Do bear in mind that your training plan needs to be sufficiently flexible to enable you to address emerging targets on a week-by-week basis. Remember that your training plan is a working document.

Working with your mentors and others

During your placement you should work with your mentors to identify key targets for your own professional development. This places an onus on you to be prepared to listen to and act on advice. You should be willing to accept advice from your more experienced colleagues. During tutorial sessions your progress will be reviewed. You should be willing to make a note of any advice you are given in these meetings and ensure that you follow it up. Outstanding trainees take seriously their emerging professional needs. They are willing to address targets and provide appropriate evidence that targets have been identified, acted upon and evaluated. Outstanding trainees are able to demonstrate that they have the professional insight to identify their own strengths and areas for development. The ability to articulate these yourself is a key professional skill that you are expected to demonstrate.

During your placement you will also work with other practitioners in school. It is likely that you will work closely with support staff and other specialist colleagues. It is important that you engage in professional dialogue about your own practice with these colleagues as well as your mentor(s). These colleagues may be able to help you reflect on your own practice and identify new targets for your development. Spend time observing teachers across the school and try to observe subject leaders teaching their subjects. If you have a specific weakness with phonics, for example, you might find it useful to observe a colleague who is skilled in teaching this aspect of the curriculum.

Consulting your learners about your teaching is a valuable strategy for helping you to reflect on your own practice. This can be done informally through the use of a suggestion box in the classroom or formally through the use of focus groups or questionnaires. The process of involving children in evaluating your practice demonstrates that you have a commitment to the principle of giving children a voice. This is a fundamental aspect of the current policy agenda.

Self-study

Throughout your placement some of your targets (either initial targets or emerging ones) may be met through self-study. You can enhance your knowledge through access to books, academic and professional journals, and using the internet. These resources can help you to address targets related to the professional standards, including helping you to develop your subject knowledge. Professional journals in particular are very useful as they usually include articles on current practice and initiatives, as well as providing case studies of good practice. In addition literature provided by your teaching unions may also be very helpful. The *Times Educational Supplement* (TES) provides a wealth of useful articles on issues related to assessment, teaching, classroom management and subject knowledge. Teachers' TV is another useful rich source of information. The Teachers' TV website enables you to download and watch videos relating to any aspect of teaching. Additionally the National Strategies website provides valuable information on many aspects of teaching, as does the Teacher Training Resource Bank website. The links to these sites can be found at the end of this chapter.

Participating in professional on-line communities

Participating in on-line communities provides you with an opportunity to join specific forums, ask questions of colleagues, share ideas and resources, and gain on-line support to enable you to address your own professional targets. The Times Education supplement website includes a number of forums related to teaching but also includes a specific forum for trainee teachers. This is a useful way of communicating with other trainee teachers and there is also a facility on this forum which enables you to consult with a teacher training expert.

When participating in on-line communities it is important to remember never to name schools, teachers, children or tutors. This would constitute a breach of your professional code of conduct. The safety and well-being of children and young people should be paramount and must never be jeopardised.

Working within a cluster

During your professional training you should create opportunities to work with colleagues to facilitate the sharing of practice. You might want to work within a cluster where a group of trainees meet regularly to share experiences and resources and to offer advice to members of the cluster. This cluster could work virtually or meet at regular intervals on a face-to-face basis. Working in this way evidences that you take your professional learning seriously and that you are willing to support colleagues in their professional development. Additionally you could ask school-based colleagues if there are any cluster groups operating within your school or between schools and whether it would be appropriate for you to join these.

 Case study

Alisha was undertaking her second teaching placement. One of her key professional targets was to develop her knowledge and understanding of assessment in KS1. The school had recently begun to use the APP materials produced by the National Strategies and had just started to use the APP materials in speaking and listening.

The KS1 colleagues had formed a cluster group to moderate assessments across the team. The team met regularly to scrutinise assessment evidence and check for parity in judgements. One cluster meeting was taking place at the start of Alisha's placement and the group had decided to look at assessments in children's writing. Alisha had identified that she lacked confidence in making judgements about children's writing. She approached the cluster lead to ask if

(Continued)

(Continued)

she would be able to attend the meeting. The team was delighted that Alisha had shown an interest in assessment and was keen for her to be involved. However, they stressed to Alisha that it was not an expert group but a learning community where all opinions and professional dialogue were valued.

Alisha attended the cluster group meeting and through professional dialogue she developed her understanding of how to analyse children's writing. She worked with a colleague in the cluster to make judgements on two pieces of work, and then they compared their judgements with the original judgements made by the class teacher. There was a difference of opinion in relation to the judgements and this led into further professional dialogue with the class teacher. This helped to clarify Alisha's understanding of the assessment process. Working further with her partner in the cluster, together they identified two key targets that the children needed to work on in relation to the samples of work they had scrutinised.

Reflection

> How was this process beneficial for Alisha?
> What other clusters might teachers be part of?

Subject/specialist associations

Subject or specialist associations are a useful way of developing your subject knowledge. Examples of these include:

> The Association for Science Education – www.ase.org.uk/home/;
> The Historical Association – www.history.org.uk/;
> Geographical Association – www.geography.org.uk/;
> National Association of Special Educational Needs – www.nasen.org.uk/;
> The Design and Technology Association – www.data.org.uk/;
> The British Association for Early Childhood Education – www.early-education. org.uk/.

These organisations are useful as they often produce professional journals which include information related to current practice within the subject/specialist area. There may be subscription charges to pay to join the organisation but the benefits often outweigh the costs. Membership of an organisation can often lead to access to resources and on-line communities. If you have a specific interest in a particular field, joining the relevant association might be a useful way of developing innovative approaches to teaching and learning. Outstanding trainees are willing to share resources and practice freely with their school-based colleagues.

Attending conferences, seminars and education exhibitions

As part of a learning community you must be responsible for identifying conferences, seminars and education exhibitions which will support you in your professional development. These are organised by a wide range of professional bodies and are usually advertised in the TES as well as on-line. Many of these facilities are free. You will have the opportunity to purchase resources and access seminars, some of which are free although you may be asked to pay a fee to attend others. Conferences, seminars and education exhibitions will introduce you to current initiatives as well as innovative practices. Ensure that you disseminate the knowledge and understanding you have gained through these professional development opportunities to colleagues. Sharing new ideas is energising for everyone concerned.

Visiting other schools

Visiting other schools which demonstrate innovative practice is an excellent way of furthering your own professional development. Your ITT provider should be able to put you in touch with schools which demonstrate specific strengths in specific areas. Your placement school may also have links with other schools which demonstrate innovative practice within specific areas. In order to address your training targets you might want to consider visiting another school to observe good practice. There is an onus on you to make contact with the school and explain the purpose of your visit. There is also an expectation that you will be willing to share the practice you have observed with colleagues in your own school.

Case study

Alex was placed in the EYFS for his second teaching placement. His previous placement was in KS2. His class mentor was also new to the Foundation Stage and was keen to develop her knowledge further.

(Continued)

(Continued)

Alex approached his ITT provider and asked for help in identifying a leading Foundation Stage teacher. His provider supplied details of an outstanding practitioner who was closely involved with the course on a strategic level. Alex contacted the practitioner to ask if it was possible to arrange a visit to her setting. He also asked if it would be acceptable to attend with his class mentor. The practitioner was more than happy to oblige and a meeting was set up during the school day so that both Alex and his class mentor could see the setting in operation.

During the visit both Alex and his class mentor were able to discuss systems of classroom organisation and they had the opportunity to observe effective practice. They were particularly keen to learn about a planning board which the leading practitioner had developed in her setting. This board enabled children to identify self-chosen activities within a given range during children's 'planning time'. It also provided a visual record of where children were working in the setting. The system was particularly effective because it ensured that by the end of a given period all children had accessed all areas of provision in the setting. During subsequent 'planning times' the children selected different cards for the planning board, thus ensuring their access to a broad and balanced curriculum.

Alex and his class mentor discussed whether they could adopt such a system in their setting. Alex was willing to trial the use of a planning board during his placement as a system for classroom organisation and his mentor encouraged him to do so. After discussions, Alex involved the whole Foundation Stage team in setting up the planning board and after a week it was reviewed and slight changes were made. The system was embedded into practice and the children responded positively to it.

Reflection

> How did Alex facilitate shared professional development with his class mentor?
> How might you benefit from visiting other schools before or during your placement?
> What potential challenges might you encounter?

Sharing professional knowledge

As a trainee teacher you are being welcomed into a learning community. You should be willing to learn from others and listen to and act upon advice. However, there will be times when you are in a position where you can share your own knowledge with school-based colleagues. You may learn many things from observing a range of teachers, accessing centre-based training, visiting other schools or from other trainees. You are in a fortunate position in that you will experience a range of schools and teachers. Your mentor(s) may have worked in the same school for some time. You therefore possess a wealth of professional experience which you can bring to your placement. You should be willing to share your knowledge with colleagues in your school but you will need to think carefully about ways in which you do this so that you do not appear to be arrogant.

Participating in training

Outstanding trainees are eager to engage in professional training to further their own professional development. Consequently you should ensure that you take part in team meetings or staff meetings and you should volunteer to participate in school-based INSET.

Sometimes it may be possible for you to 'tap into' CPD training that is being accessed by your school-based colleagues. Many teachers and members of support staff attend after-school courses, network meetings and briefing meetings and some of these are free of charge. It may be possible for you to gain permission to accompany school-based colleagues to these professional development opportunities.

There is now increasing use being made of on-line training courses. For example some local authorities run free on-line training on safeguarding and e-safety. The National Strategies website provides on-line training on aspects related to inclusion. These training opportunities will provide you with valuable information that may inform your own professional practice.

Identifying longer-term career goals

At the end of your professional training your ITT provider will support you in identifying targets for your induction year using the *Career Entry Development Profile*. Outstanding trainees will still have targets that they want to focus on. They are reflective professionals and they recognise their strengths and development needs.

In order to remain challenged and interested throughout your teaching career you should continually set yourself new targets. These can be:

> broad targets – yearly targets;
> medium-term targets – either termly or half-termly targets;
> short-term targets – weekly/daily targets.

Setting yourself new targets and taking ownership of your own professional development will help you to be an effective teacher. Continually engaging in a process of reflection–plan–do–review will help you to maintain your motivation during even the most challenging times.

Professional development

Browse the trainee teacher forums on the TES website. Go to www.tes.co.uk/community.aspx?navcode=14.

Join the forums and take part in the discussions.

Link to research

Hustler et al. (2003) found that most teachers thought about professional development in terms of attending courses, conferences and INSET. The research found that few teachers participated in research, award-bearing courses and international visits, although these were valued.

> What benefits can research-based professional development activities bring to your practice?
> How might you engage with research-based professional development?

Further reading

Stoll, L., Wallace, M., Bolam, R., McMahon, A., Thomas, S., Hawkey, K., Smith, M. and Greenwood, A. (2003) *Creating and Sustaining Effective Professional Learning Communities,* DfES Research Brief RBX12-03. Nottingham: DfES Publications.
This research report discusses the characteristics of a Professional Learning Community and how this is applied to a school context.

Useful websites

www.tes.co.uk/home.aspx
www.ttrb.ac.uk/
nationalstrategies.standards.dcsf.gov.uk/
www.teachers.tv/
www.history.org.uk/
www.geography.org.uk/
www.earlyyearseducator.co.uk/
www.tes.co.uk/
www.nasen.org.uk/
www.ase.org.uk/

These websites will enable you to access resources to support planning and teaching and some of the sites provide forums through which you can communicate with colleagues. This will facilitate the development of reflective practice.

9

Organising your files

This chapter covers

This chapter offers guidance on organising your placement files. We wish to stress that this is only one suggested model. Your ITT provider may have a specific format for you to follow and, if so, you should adhere to this. Your files provide you with the opportunity to evidence your achievements against both the QTS standards and the Ofsted criteria for evaluating trainees' performance. The documentation and evidence within your files will be carefully scrutinised by school mentors and provider link tutors. School-based mentors will already have a very clear, sound knowledge and understanding of your performance against the standards. However, it is your responsibility to ensure that high quality files convey this evidence to your provider link tutor. Final judgements about your performance are made by both the school and your ITT provider. Many aspects of your performance will not have been observed by your provider link tutor and consequently your school-based training files provide a crucial source of evidence and support effective moderation between the ITT provider and the school.

The school-based training files provide an opportunity for you to evidence your progress towards many of the QTS standards. For the purposes of this chapter we have selected the standards relating to planning, assessment, team working and evaluation of your practice.

A suggested model for structuring your file(s)

You must be aware of the need to adhere to the safeguarding policies stipulated by both your ITT provider and the school you are working in. It is essential that you comply with these policies and you must familiarise yourself with

Table 9.1 Suggested framework for organising your files

Section	Title	Content
Contents Page		
1	Personal Information and Initial Action Plan	> Curriculum Vitae > Letter of introduction to the school > Previous placement report if applicable > Placement action plan with clear targets > Pre-placement checklists to be included
2	School Information	> Summary of inspection findings from the latest Ofsted report > School prospectus > Key policies – behaviour, marking, equal opportunities, safeguarding, health and safety, and child protection (trainees may prefer to keep a separate file for policies) > List of key personnel, roles and responsibilities > School timetable > Notes from school induction
3	Class Information	> Class list in alphabetical order > Class grouping arrangements > Classroom plan > Class timetable > Prior assessments of learners > Details about individual pupils, including copies of individual education plans > Information about class routines and systems > Information about the roles and responsibilities of support staff > Notes from class induction > Long-term plan to show curriculum coverage

(Continued)

Table 9.1 (Continued)

Section	Title	Content
4	Medium-Term Planning	> Medium-term plans/unit plans to show coverage of objectives in all curriculum areas during your placement > Weekly teaching timetable
5	Short-Term Planning, Evaluations and Record Keeping	> Weekly planning > Lesson plans for every taught lesson arranged in date order > Evaluations for every taught lesson at the end of each lesson plan > Briefing sheets for support staff > Assessment records after each lesson, e.g. whole-class record sheets, traffic light systems > End-of-week evaluations with clear targets identified for the following week
6	Feedback and Action Planning	> Lesson observation feedback arranged chronologically > Periodic reviews of progress > End of placement report > End of placement action plan
7	Assessment	> Samples of marked work/observations of children > Group assessments > Samples of moderated assessments
8	Initial Professional Development	> Observations of other lessons across the school > Handouts from staff meetings or training days > Record of directed tasks and evidence of completion of these > Synoptic critical reflection

them before you begin to compile your teaching files. For this reason the model shown in Figure 9.1 is a suggested framework for organising your file. Ensure that you ask your provider and your school for advice regarding safeguarding.

You may find it useful to create two separate files due to the amount of paper work which you will generate during your block placement. One file can be used to store planning and evaluations and the other file can be used to store your assessments of your learners' progress. This should make the process more manageable and the paperwork will be more accessible to your mentors and tutors.

Personal information and initial action plan

You should send a letter of introduction to the head teacher of your placement school and a copy of this should be stored in the first section of your placement file. We cannot stress too strongly that spelling, grammar and punctuation should be precise. Errors at this stage will not create a good impression. In the letter you should:

> acknowledge your appreciation that the school has offered you a trainee placement;
> outline your achievements, referring to previous placements if applicable;
> demonstrate that you have undertaken personal research relating to the school and highlight the reasons why you are enthusiastic about your placement there;
> identify key targets that you hope to address during your placement;
> confirm the dates of prior visits as well as the placement dates.

You will require an updated curriculum vitae. A copy of this should be forwarded to the placement school with the introductory letter and a copy should also be held in your file. This should be a positive document which celebrates your achievements. You will need to include key information such as:

> your name, gender and contact details;
> your educational history (starting from primary school and working towards your present education);
> qualifications (most recent first);
> your employment history;
> placement experiences and experience of voluntary work if applicable;

> personal interests;
> key skills which you possess;
> possibly a photograph but this is not essential.

This will provide the school with contextual information about you and will enable them to begin preparations to address your specific interests and needs.

We cannot over-emphasise the importance of presenting your placement school with your current action plan. This should outline the key targets that you hope to address during your placement. Formats for recording key targets will be supplied by your ITT provider. Previous placement reports will provide your mentors with detailed information about your achievements and developing needs as a trainee teacher. We acknowledge that trainees may be reluctant to share negative information with a receiving placement school. Although we fully understand these anxieties, it is in your best interests to share all information from the beginning of your placement. Bear in mind that the school in which you are placed has elected to support a trainee teacher. Trainee teachers are not qualified, experienced teachers and you will not be expected to be fully competent in all areas. We emphasise the need for you to be open and honest from the beginning. This should be beneficial to you as the school will then be able to support your individual needs from the outset. Do not leave mentors to discover your needs. This wastes time and prevents them from supporting you effectively from the outset. You may feel that your previous placement report contains inaccuracies regarding your achievement and for this reason you may be reluctant to share it with your new school. Be assured that any inaccuracies will be quickly identified if this is the case. Honesty really is the best policy.

School information

You will require key information before you begin your placement to provide you with an understanding of the context in which you will be working. Initially it is essential that you locate and download the most recent inspection report relating to the school. This will inform you of both the strengths and identified areas for development in relation to the school. The head teacher may be willing to share the current school improvement plans with you. This must not be an expectation on your behalf but if you are able to either gain access to it or to discuss the key points identified in the plan you will find this very useful information. The school improvement plans will identify the key targets relating to the school's future development and will reflect inspection findings and rigorous analysis of pupil data. Schools will be taking steps to achieve these broad targets and you should be familiar with the strategies employed by the school to address these. As a trainee teacher you have a responsibility to adhere to school priorities and you must focus on these as you consider planning, teaching, learning and assessment.

Key school policies will also be vital in ensuring that you adhere to the agreed practices of the school. You will not need to request a copy of every school policy. However, you must be familiar with policies relating to e-safety, safeguarding and health and safety in addition to policies relating to teaching, learning, behaviour management and assessment. In addition many settings have specific risk assessments and you should be familiar with and adhere to these. Discuss with the head teacher and/or mentors the policies which you will need to reflect in your practices. Obtain a copy of the relevant policies, read them carefully and keep them in your file for future reference. Remember that your practices should accurately reflect the policies.

During your induction to the school seek to acquire a copy of the school prospectus. This holds additional information about general school routines and the roles and responsibilities of key personnel across the school. These professionals should be familiar to you as they will be able to support you in specific areas of your training throughout your school-based placement. Additionally ensure that you ask for a copy of the whole-school timetable. This usually includes the times of the school day, break times, assembly times and allocated use of shared teaching areas.

During your induction you will gather a wealth of information. You may have further questions and you should not hesitate to pursue these. Useful questions may include the following.

> What is the policy for entering and exiting the school?
> What are the arrangements for children entering and leaving the building?
> Where are the emergency exits and what are are the procedures during a fire drill?
> Is there a dress code for staff?
> What times are you expected to arrive and leave school?
> Are trainee teachers welcomed in the staffroom?
> Are trainee teachers expected to attend staff meetings and other professional development activities?
> Are trainee teachers allowed access to school policies?
> Are there any whole-school approaches for managing children's behaviour?
> What are the procedures for reporting accidents involving children?

> Who are the qualified first aiders?
> What is the policy of the school in relation to the administration of pre-
  scribed medicines?
> What is the school policy regarding photographing children?
> What is the school policy regarding safe use of the internet?
> What ICT facilities are available to support learning and teaching?
> How do trainee teachers access the ICT network?
> What other resources are available to support learning and teaching and
  where are these stored?
> What are the procedures for obtaining resources?
> Is there a policy for the use of the photocopier?
> How are support staff deployed throughout the school?
> What intervention programmes are used to support specific groups of learners
  throughout the school?
> What are the arrangements for parental access to the building?
> Is there a school and/or class timetable?
> Is there a whole-school approach to planning? If so, must this be followed or
  are you able to use the planning sheets suggested by the university?
> How is the curriculum organised in the school?
> Where will you be able to access information relating to learners' current
  attainment?
> How are registers completed?
> How is money collected from children?

You may have additional questions and if they are relevant to your practice you
should not hesitate to ask them. You will be expected to keep a record of the
information you have acquired. Place this in your file for ongoing reference.
This is not an exhaustive list and you may have other questions which you
should not be afraid to ask.

Class information

During your induction to the class it is important that you acquire a range of
vital information to develop your familiarity with routines, systems and expectations to support you in your placement. You will have questions at this stage
which may include the following.

> Is there a class list?
> What are the grouping arrangements for different aspects of learning?
> Is there a plan of the classroom?

> Do you have permission to take photographs of the classroom environment?
> Is there a class timetable?
> What resources are available in the classroom and how are they stored?
> What are the roles and responsibilities of the support staff you will be working with?
> How are support staff currently deployed?
> How is access to the curriculum managed?
> Is current assessment data available for individual learners?
> Are details regarding learners' specific medical, social, emotional, behavioural and learning needs available?
> What specific routines and systems operate in this class?
> Is a long-term curriculum plan available?
> What specific interventions operate to support individuals or groups of learners? Who are these learners?

During the class induction ensure that you document the information you gain and keep a copy of this information in your file for future reference. Be aware that schools operate policies to safeguard children. You may not be permitted to store information regarding individual children in your placement school. It is essential that you adhere to such policies and address any difficulties with the head teacher and your ITT provider.

Medium-term planning

Medium-term plans should outline the knowledge, skills and understanding that you intend to teach your learners throughout the duration of the placement. The purpose of these plans is to enable you to demonstrate your ability to plan for progression within specific subjects or areas of learning. The plans should outline effective sequences of learning when planning a series of lessons. You will need to produce medium-term plans for specific areas of the curriculum that you will be teaching. Medium-term planning provides a broad overview of the purposes of lessons and the ways in which these will be addressed. Adhere to school policies in relation to medium-term planning to facilitate your work.

In some schools medium-term plans will already be in place. In such circumstances ensure that you obtain a copy of these as you must plan from them. In other schools it will be your responsibility to formulate medium-term plans. You should seek guidance from your class mentor to do so as your mentor will be familiar with the intended learning.

Where plans are available such documentation is rarely totally rigid. This provides you with an opportunity to demonstrate your ability to be innovative when planning a scheme of work. Outstanding trainees are able to 'show innovation within the constraints of a scheme of work/curriculum' (Ofsted, 2009: 32). It is important that you adhere to the intended learning objectives identified on a medium-term plan. However, you have the opportunity to consider developing innovative approaches to address the intended learning. Outstanding trainees demonstrate 'innovative approaches to the integration of Every Child Matters and social and cultural diversity' (Ofsted, 2009: 32). Additionally they should 'show innovative and creative thinking – lateral thinkers' (Ofsted, 2009: 36). Innovative approaches for teaching have been discussed in Chapter 4. Taking ownership of the medium-term planning process will afford you the chance to demonstrate your creativity. Capitalise on this opportunity.

The curriculum areas that you will be teaching will need to be identified in collaboration with your class mentor. You should draw up a clear timetable for your placement. This should show a weekly overview of the curriculum areas you will be teaching and times when you have responsibility for the class. You should also identify times when you will be formally observed as well as time allocated for planning, preparation and assessment. Additionally you will require dedicated time for professional development. Your mentors will be able to support you in planning effective professional development opportunities to address your individual targets as identified on your action plan.

Short-term planning, evaluations and record keeping

During your placement you will be required to complete weekly and daily lesson plans. These must demonstrate your ability to plan for progression and must also evidence your ability to plan lessons which meet the needs of individuals and groups of learners. These expectations must be evident on all planning documentation. Ofsted requires that you 'demonstrate a clear and deep understanding of how to plan for progression – stages in learning, different rates of progress, identifying clear "strands of progression" and the use of these to plan "steps in learning", their teaching, dealing with barriers to learning, and through this demonstrate depth of subject knowledge and subject pedagogy' (2009: 32). Chapter 3 supports you in addressing this expectation.

Your files are working documents and should reflect your understanding and ability to respond to lesson outcomes. It will be necessary to annotate your plans in light of the assessment process during and at the end of all lessons. Outstanding trainees 'maintain files as working documents – annotated as part of self-evaluation' (Ofsted, 2009: 32). Consequently you will be expected to evidence the ways in which medium- and short-term planning have been adapted to address the emerging needs of your learners.

High quality reflection is of paramount importance in enabling you to evaluate the impact of your teaching on the progress of all learners. It is essential that every lesson is carefully evaluated by you to identify both the strengths in your teaching and areas requiring further development. The emphasis of these evaluations must be placed on the quality of pupils' learning within a lesson. Identified targets should enable you to ensure that all learners make good/outstanding progress. Lesson evaluations should evidence critical and rigorous reflection with a clear focus on the learning which is taking place. Outstanding trainees 'show high quality self-evaluation with clear focus on learners …' (Ofsted, 2009: 32).

End-of-week evaluations must evidence rigorous reflection on the learning that has taken place each week with clearly identified targets for the following week. There should be evidence that you have implemented strategies to address your targets and acted on advice from your mentors and tutors. Outstanding trainees set 'challenging targets for their own professional development … with evidence of implementation and further review and critical analysis and reflection, taking full account of feedback from trainers and other professionals they work with' (Ofsted, 2009: 32).

Your file should show secure evidence of the individual attainment of learners at the end of lessons. Approaches to record individual assessments are discussed in Chapter 5. Assessment records should give a clear picture of all learners' achievements and needs and you must demonstrate how your assessments have contributed to subsequent plans. Your annotations on your planning should evidence this clearly.

Ensure that all support staff and adult helpers have a clear understanding of learning intentions and the ways in which these will be addressed in advance of a lesson. You need to develop systems to enable support staff and other adults to effectively communicate learning outcomes to you when they have been responsible for working with individuals and groups of learners. Ensure that they are familiar with and are able to complete assessment records provided by you.

Feedback and action planning

You will need to create a section in your file to store feedback following formal observations and periodic feedback. Periodic feedback includes end-of-week feedback or feedback at the midpoint of the placement. The records of feedback provide an important source of evidence to your provider link tutor about targets that you have been set during the placement and whether these have been addressed.

In addition to written commentaries on your progress you will receive additional and frequent verbal feedback. There will be an expectation that you will be able to reflect accurately on your own achievements and that you will also be able to identify areas in which you must further develop your skills, knowledge and understanding as a teacher.

We argue that outstanding trainees will have a clear professional insight into the quality of their teaching. However, you may receive outstanding feedback but you should still carefully consider the ways in which you can demonstrate further progress. Listen carefully to advice and feedback, which should be well considered by you. Engage actively with the feedback and ask questions that you feel will support your progress. This should help to clarify your thinking. Feedback will hopefully be positive and constructive. However, there will be occasions when minor concerns could be raised. Remember at all times to conduct yourself in a professional manner when engaging with school-based colleagues. You should welcome the advice you are given, listen to it and act upon it.

Targets will be set periodically for you during the placement. You need to provide documentary evidence in your file that:

> targets have been set and agreed by you;
> strategies have been implemented to address these targets;
> you have reviewed your progress towards these targets;
> you have evidenced your achievement towards these targets.

You need to develop clear documentation to demonstrate your engagement with the target setting and review process. Outstanding trainees 'have the ability to reflect critically and rigorously on their own practice to inform their professional development, and to take and evaluate appropriate actions – they are able to learn from their mistakes' (Ofsted, 2009: 36). Additionally outstanding trainees 'take full responsibility for their own professional development' (Ofsted, 2009: 36).

Assessment

The complexities of assessment are discussed in Chapter 5. Your ability to fulfil all the requirements of assessment must be clearly evidenced in your assessment file and will include evidence of:

> marked samples of work;
> observational assessments of individuals and groups;
> records of group and individual attainment in the curriculum areas you have taught;
> annotated photographs;
> digital records;
> examples of target setting for groups and individuals;
> attainment tracking sheets;
> evaluation of pupils' progress against targets set.

You will need to demonstrate your ability to make accurate judgements about children's learning. In addition you will need to show how your assessments have impacted on subsequent planning. Your ITT provider and school mentors will provide additional guidance on specific formats for recording progress. You will need to take account of the assessment and feedback policy in the school, ensuring that you adhere to specific requirements. You will also need to work within the school's target setting policy. Outstanding trainees 'provide evidence of monitoring and recording learners' progress and how the outcomes are used in subsequent planning, with a clear focus on groups and individual learners' (Ofsted, 2009: 32).

Initial professional development

Create a section in your file to evidence the professional development tasks which you have undertaken during your placement. These could include:

> observations of teaching, learning and classroom management across the life of the school;
> completion of directed tasks specified by your ITT provider or tasks which were designed to meet your individual training needs;
> notes from training opportunities;
> outcomes of visits to other schools.

You should reflect on what you have learnt following these professional development tasks and identify ways in which this training has impacted on your practice. Produce accounts of what you have observed or discussed with other colleagues and demonstrate the ways in which you have included this in your own practice.

At the end of your placement some ITT providers may require you to produce a synoptic critical reflection. This should identify your strengths, significant achievements, areas for development and personal philosophy of education. Your own values about teaching and learning should be expressed and supported by reference to both educational theory and practice. This reflective task at the end of your placement will evidence your ability to link theory and practice.

📁   **Case study**

Tom was a trainee teacher on his final placement. The file from his previous placement was exemplary. Before his final placement he sought support from his ITT provider to develop his ability to evidence his contribution towards whole-school targets. Tom scrutinised a range of school documentation, including the latest inspection report, the school development plan and action plans. When he had familiarised himself with the school targets he transferred these to a simple grid. As he began his placement Tom discussed with his mentor ways in which he could address the school targets. Next to each target he documented evidence of the ways in which he addressed the targets. A further column enabled him to review progress towards the targets. Tom also adopted a similar approach for identifying, addressing and reviewing his own targets. Both documents constituted outstanding evidence for the provider link tutor of the ways in which Tom had acknowledged and acted upon identified targets.

It is notable that the documentation developed by Tom was clear and simple but extremely effective. Documentation does not need to be onerous.

Reflection

> Consider ways in which you can have ownership of your own file.
> Consider the ways in which you can present information in a simple and clear format.

Professional development

Arrange an opportunity with your ITT provider to scrutinise the files of other trainee teachers. Refer to the model suggested in this chapter to support you in evaluating and identifying files or parts of files which demonstrate outstanding qualities.

Link to research

Rawlings identifies specific reflective practitioner skills. These include:

> knowledge of self and others;
> personal philosophies;
> management of self and working with others;
> knowledge and understanding of the child;
> use of technology;
> ability to develop research questions;
> conflict management;
> recognising one's own strengths and areas for development;
> self-evaluation;
> questioning your certainties (Malaguzzi, 1993);
> ability to value self and others;
> managing change;
> empathy;
> ability to listen;
> effective communication;
> ability to collaborate and problem solve;
> equal opportunities;
> ability to recognise one's own and others' triggers for powerful feelings;
> study;
> time management;
> curiosity, motivation and creativity;
> work, rest and time to relax. (2008: 23)

These skills provide you with useful points of consideration when you complete your synoptic critical reflection. At the end of your placement identify the areas that you need to reflect upon using the above list. Identify your strengths and areas for development. Your file should demonstrate your ability to reflect on your overall

(Continued)

(Continued)

development during and at the end of your placement. Your ability to demonstrate reflective practice will emerge through daily, weekly and periodic self-evaluations of your progress. In addition your ability to be a reflective practitioner will be evident in the plan–do–review process. This process is central to your development and clear documentation should evidence your ability to set targets, take action, review progress and set new targets. The above points for reflection could be considered in a post-placement tutorial with your personal/academic tutor.

Further reading

Medwell, J. (2007) *Successful Teaching Placement: Primary and Early Years*, 2nd edn. Exeter: Learning Matters.
This text provides comprehensive guidance on managing the day-to-day challenges of a teaching placement. It provides practical advice and is both accessible and informative.

10

Going beyond the standards

This chapter covers

Throughout the training process you will have initially enjoyed the support of your training provider and school-based mentors. As your knowledge, skills and understandings have developed you will have become increasingly reflective and so will have developed a clearer and stronger professional identity. As an outstanding trainee you will now be familiar with, and capable of, evidencing your ability to demonstrate the full scope of all the professional competencies for QTS. In moving beyond these competencies you will need to work with much greater independence. To do so you must consider the development of your own systems, initiatives and ideas. Such innovations clearly need to be discussed with your school-based mentors and other colleagues. In this way you will be driving your own practices and those of others. It will be necessary for you to articulate and justify such innovations and to realise that some, but not all, will be accepted. In working in collaboration with other colleagues you must be prepared to develop your initial ideas with them and to make adaptations to enhance your original proposals. Once you have implemented innovations you must reflect upon the benefits of these to your learners and your practices, keeping an open mind to ensure that they do enhance teaching and learning.

In this chapter we suggest ways in which outstanding trainees can begin to move beyond the requirements of the QTS professional competencies. We have identified key professional competencies which will exemplify the ways in which you can begin to challenge your own practices. We acknowl- edge that reflective and creative trainees will have their own ideas for developing aspects of their practice.

Recognise and respect the contribution that colleagues, parents and carers can make to the development and well-being of children and young people and to raising their levels of attainment

To further enhance your practice we suggest that you focus on developing partnerships with parents and carers. This is a fundamental strand of current policy agenda. The following ideas may support you in addressing this.

> Develop a learning wall on which you identify the weekly intended learning outcomes for groups of learners. This resource will be particularly effective in informing parents and carers of younger children, who often come into school on a daily basis, of the learning which is taking place during the week. Ensure that this information is replicated onto a newsletter and/or school website/virtual learning environment to ensure that it is accessible to all parents/carers and all age groups.
> Ensure that parents and carers are familiar with broad learning intentions for class topics or thematic work in advance of your placement. These can be communicated through newsletters, information booklets, the school website or virtual learning environment. It may be useful to suggest the ways in which parents or carers may work with their children at home to support their learning.
> Workshops are another way in which you can communicate with parents and carers. Workshops could focus on sharing broad intended learning for a theme or topic. Additionally workshops may focus on specific learning needs or initiatives for groups of learners. Through these workshops you can communicate key learning targets to parents and carers and identify practical suggestions for ways in which they can support their child's learning at home.
> Within a class there will be individual children with specific learning needs. This could include children with English as an additional language, children with special educational needs as well as children who are gifted and talented. Develop resources to support their home learning and identify opportunities to meet with parents/carers of these children to share your suggestions and resources (standards related to personalised learning can also be further developed in this way).

Case study

Ben was teaching a class of Reception children in the early stages of their education. Through his assessments in phonics Ben immediately noticed that children were articulating the phonemes incorrectly. Ben knew that it was important for both school and home to work together to support the children. He identified the need to work with parents to ensure that they were able to articulate the phonemes correctly themselves. Ben organised a workshop and invited parents and carers to attend. He used the training materials from the *Letters and Sounds* DVD to demonstrate correct articulation of phonemes. He explained to parents the ways in which early reading and writing is supported through a programme of synthetic phonics. Ben supplied each parent with a copy of the *Letters and Sounds* DVD to ensure that they could refer to it to develop their own accurate articulation of the phonemes.

Reflection

> In what other ways could you address misconceptions of parents and carers through the use of a workshop?

This case study provides an example of excellent practice, although you might not have the time or be able to secure the permission to orchestrate this level of parental involvement. Nevertheless you could experiment with approaches like this during your NQT year. If your class mentor provides any workshops for parents it might be useful for you to offer support in delivering the workshop, perhaps through co-presenting the session. You will need to ensure that you have a secure knowledge of the content that you are presenting to parents and also be confident in your presentational skills.

Have a commitment to collaboration and co-operative working

To further enhance your practice we would suggest that you inform parents and carers of learning intentions prior to beginning your placement. Take this opportunity to acknowledge to parents and carers that they may have specific knowledge, skills and understanding which could enhance the children's learning. Suggestions can be made by you but you must make it clear that your ideas are not exhaustive. Invite parents and carers to identify their personal skills, knowledge and understanding and encourage them to work alongside you in sharing their expertise to enhance teaching and learning within your classroom.

Reflect on and improve their practice, and take responsibility for identifying and meeting their developing professional needs

The current educational policy agenda promotes children's participation in all aspects of their education. To further enhance your practice consider ways in which you will engage children in supporting you to reflect on and improve your own practice. You can consult children about your teaching and their learning in different ways, which may include:

> questionnaires to elicit children's views in relation to your teaching at the end of lessons and periodically during your placement;
> focus groups to discuss which aspects of your teaching they enjoy and aspects which could be improved;
> a suggestions box in the classroom which enables children to post their views about your teaching – this would need to be confidential and anonymous.

Have a creative and constructively critical approach towards innovation, being prepared to adapt their practice where benefits and improvements are identified

As an outstanding trainee you will have begun a never ending journey in which you continually strive to enhance your practices. This can be achieved in the following ways.

> It is your professional responsibility to engage with current innovations to support practices. Until this point other professionals will have familiarised you with current development in early years and primary education. You will continue to learn about innovative developments in teaching and learning through colleagues, centre-based training and professional development. In addition to this outstanding trainees will independently research initiatives to support their practices.

> As a reflective practitioner you will encounter barriers to the learning of individuals and groups of learners. It is on such occasions that independent research can support you in developing innovative approaches to break down these barriers. As a practitioner researcher you will frequently engage in a cycle of action research to enhance teaching and learning. This involves a process of identifying problems or issues related to teaching and learning. You will then research into possible innovations or solutions to address the problem. You will adopt carefully selected innovations and evaluate the impact of these on your learners. You will then evaluate the suitability of the innovations and make a professional decision as to whether you continue with them, adapt them or discard them. Action research is most effective when colleagues are participants in the process. You may have identified the issues and researched into possible innovations but from this point in the process it is always more beneficial to engage with other professionals in the implementation and evaluation of chosen initiatives. Outstanding trainees will demonstrate leadership skills and steer the process.

Case study

Sasha was a trainee working with Year 1 children in an inner city school. The development of writing amongst boys had been identified as a priority for school improvement. Data indicated that the attainment levels of 90 per cent of the boys in the class in which she was working were below national expectations. Her observations indicated that many of the boys were reluctant to write for a range of purposes. Sasha researched strategies to support and motivate boys to write. A relative of one of the children in the class was a car mechanic. Sasha arranged for the mechanic to bring a car into school to develop the curiosity of the boys in particular. Under supervision the children explored the car in small groups. The boys responded well to this and it was notable that they were curious and began to pose questions. These were answered effectively by the mechanic. Following this experience Sasha arranged to visit the garage. She used a camcorder to record images of the working garage and she interviewed several members of staff about their roles. The recording also focused on the purposes of writing within the garage. These included:

> recording appointments;
> recording telephone messages;
> completing service records;

(Continued)

(Continued)

> completing order forms;
> bills;
> environmental print in the garage including advertisements, notices, price list.

In the classroom Sasha shared the video with the children, pointing out the purposes of writing. Sasha then created a garage with a reception area, which included a box model car made by the children. She then recreated simple forms for the children to use in the role play. The children were able to access the garage in groups. Initially they were supported by an adult who focused on opportunities and purposes for writing. The children became enthused and were eager to take on the roles of the people in the garage. In doing so they automatically began to write for a range of different purposes. These included:

> lists;
> letters;
> signs/captions;
> notes.

Reflection

> How did Sasha identify the problem?
> How did Sasha capitalise on the children's interests?
> How did Sasha address the problem in a positive way?
> How can you capitalise on children's interests in other ways to contribute to raising standards in reading, writing and mathematics?

Have a secure knowledge and understanding of their subjects/curriculum areas and related pedagogy to enable them to teach effectively across the age and ability range for which they are trained

Outstanding trainees will demonstrate a very high subject and pedagogical knowledge in all areas of the curriculum. Trainees who wish to move forward in their practice need to consider and develop opportunities for learners to apply their knowledge, skills and understanding across the breadth of the curriculum. Activities may be adult led, child initiated with adult support as well as initiated by the child without adult intervention. Opportunities to use and apply learning across the breath of the curriculum provide children with clear purposes for learning as well as opportunities to deepen their knowledge, skills and understanding.

Consider the following suggestions as a means of building upon this professional competency.

> Create opportunities in the wider learning environment for children to apply the knowledge, skills and understanding they have developed in previous learning. A lesson on money could be supported through role play, such as a class shop. This affords children the opportunity to work with money in independent activities, in activities where adults identify misconceptions and scaffold learning as well as in activities led by adults. The role play will provide a useful context to assess children's knowledge, understanding and skills. Additionally it gives children the opportunity to make sense of their learning in different contexts. A role play activity will also provide a valuable context for the application of learning from other areas of the curriculum.

> A class enterprise project will provide an opportunity for the application of learning from a range of curriculum areas. An example of this would be to create a greeting cards company which engages children in designing, creating, advertising and selling cards for different purposes. Within such a project children would be required to use the knowledge, skills and understanding they have previously been taught in English, mathematics, art and design, ICT, and design and technology. The children would also be required to use many cross-curricular key skills including problem solving, reasoning, communication, team working and collaboration to form a successful company. Enterprise projects could involve members of the local community, businesses, charities and voluntary groups. Linked learning in this way enables children to understand the purposes of learning in discrete lessons.

> Make connections between subjects. Work in history or art could complement work on symmetry in mathematics and enables children to understand the applications of specific ideas.

> Think carefully about how subjects such as geography, religious education, history, and design and technology can be used as vehicles for teaching children about 'big issues' such as sustainability, social and cultural diversity, and community cohesion.

Know how to use skills in literacy, numeracy and ICT to support their teaching and wider professional activities

As an outstanding trainee you will be confident in identifying opportunities for the use of literacy, numeracy and ICT across the wider curriculum. To further develop your progress in this professional competency you could consider the innovative use of ICT to personalise learning for children with specific needs or interests. Some children may have difficulties with literacy and may find it hard to record their ideas in writing. As a reflective practitioner you could consider how these children could use ICT to record their learning in a range of ways. Think about ways of challenging children through the innovative use of ICT. You may wish to try the following ideas:

> replace writing with digital recording, including making films and audio recordings, and access to computer software to enable children to complete specific tasks and communicate their learning;
> the use of video conferencing and blogs to support teaching and learning;
> the use of the virtual learning environment to support teaching and learning;
> the use of the school website to support teaching and learning.

Schools will have a range of ICT hardware and software. This may include animation software, palm top computers, tablet PCs, cameras, music technology, mobile access to the internet, voting pads and audio recorders. Capitalise on this by identifying the resources that are available and think creatively about the ways in which these can be integrated into teaching and learning across the full breadth of the curriculum. These suggestions will also support you further in developing your ability to design opportunities for learners to improve their literacy, numeracy and ICT skills.

Know how to make effective personalised provision for those they teach, including those for whom English is an additional language or who have special educational needs or disabilities, and how to take practical account of diversity and promote equality and inclusion in their teaching

This competency focuses on the importance of personalising learning for groups of learners and individual learners. This professional competency requires you to acknowledge and act upon children's perspectives to enhance teaching and learning. To further enhance your practice you can consider creative ways eliciting pupil voice for all learners. To go beyond the realms of the competency ensure that the systems you create are accessible to all children regardless of their abilities to communicate through spoken language. Develop systems of eliciting pupil voice which are fully inclusive. In particular reflect on your systems of providing the following children with a voice:

> children with language, communication and interaction difficulties;
> children whose first language is not English;
> children who are mute;
> children with sensory impairments.

You might consider establishing picture exchange communication systems to support learners with communication and interaction difficulties. Additionally, you may wish to access training in sign language systems to aid your communication skills with non-verbal learners. Using additional communication systems will facilitate two-way communication, thus enabling all learners to fully participate in the full life of the school.

Outstanding trainees can develop their practice further by considering creative approaches to address communication between themselves and parents and carers. These approaches will enable you to further personalise learning and may include the following:

> questionnaires to parents;
> development of focus groups to include parents and practitioners;
> suggestion box to enable parents to offer their own ideas to enhance personalised learning;
> development of home–school communication systems to facilitate dialogue between school and home, and home and school.

Plan homework and other out-of-class work to sustain learners' progress and to extend and consolidate their learning

Outstanding trainees set homework and plan out-of-class work to consolidate children's learning. The school will already have developed community links and be familiar with the ways in which the community and the school can work in partnership. However, you cannot assume that parents and carers will be familiar with the resources and facilities both in the immediate and wider community which can support learning. You can research into the availability of community resources and communicate this information to parents and carers through:

> a classroom community board;
> a parent newsletter;
> a school website;
> a virtual learning environment.

Homework provides a valuable opportunity to consolidate knowledge and skills that have previously been taught in the classroom. Through homework children can engage in creative problem solving. The following points should be considered when setting homework.

> Never assume that all children will be supported at home by parents or carers.
> Never assume that all children have access to computers, the internet or even basic resources such as pencils and paper. If tasks require the use of these resources consider ways in which the school can make provision for this.
> Young children should not be punished for failing to complete homework as it is the responsibility of parents and carers to encourage them to do so.
> Consider ways in which children can be supported in school to complete homework tasks if they cannot be completed at home.
> Not all tasks need to involve recording.
> Consider how you intend to provide children with feedback on their homework and whether this feedback will be individual or generic.
> Value children's attempts at completing homework: do not set homework and then ignore it as this will demotivate children.
> Consider the use of practical tasks rather than always requiring children to complete worksheets.
> Consider the amount of time you expect children to take in completing homework tasks.
> Consider the importance of differentiation: one set task for the whole class will not meet the needs of all of the children.
> Ensure that homework tasks do not require children to have knowledge and skills which have not been taught in lessons.

Examples of homework tasks include:

> research projects, for example to research further into aspects of class topics such as The Romans;
> completing work that has been started in class;

> a bank of literacy or mathematical games which focus on phonics or early number skills which children can play with parents – these could be rotated around the children;
> story sacks to enable children and parents to share stories together – these could be rotated around the children;
> practical tasks, for example looking for shapes in the home and local environment and taking photographs of these on a digital camera – this would link to a class topic on shape;
> handy hints sheets for parents: these information sheets inform parents and carers of the learning that has taken place in school and provide practical suggestions as to how this learning can be reinforced at home, for example a class topic on mass could be consolidated through a baking activity at home.

You can suggest ways that parents and carers might wish to use the resources in the community to support their child's current learning. Such facilities may include:

> libraries;
> museums and galleries;
> zoos;
> local events;
> community centres;
> places of worship;
> National Trust sites;
> castles;
> conservation areas;
> parks;
> sporting facilities.

Make effective use of a range of assessment, monitoring and recording strategies

An outstanding trainee will understand the assess–plan–do–review cycle which supports very effective teaching. During school-based training it is likely that you will have adopted systems and recording formats developed by your school or ITT provider. You will now have a high level of confidence, knowledge and understanding relating to assessment practices and may well consider that generic systems and formats do not fully meet your personal requirements.

Carefully consider the formats you are currently using. If these do not fully meet your needs take ownership of them by either adapting them or developing systems and formats of your own.

Support and guide learners to reflect on their learning, identify the progress they have made and identify their emerging learning needs

By now learners' self-assessment strategies should be embedded in your daily practice. In reality many self-assessment systems engage the children in reflecting upon their own achievements and conveying these through simple signals such as:

> thumbs up – *I have achieved the learning outcomes;*
> thumbs sideways – *I have partially achieved the learning outcomes;*
> thumbs down – *I need further support to achieve the learning outcomes.*

You will need to reflect upon ways in which you can further engage the children with self-assessment. However, you also need to develop systems at stages throughout the lesson and in the plenary which enable children to validate their own judgements. Fundamentally you need to know *why* children find something difficult or easy and you need to use learners' own assessments to identify misconceptions as well as their clear understandings. It is important that you ask the children to *demonstrate* their learning and understanding to enable you to build on their individual current achievements. This can be addressed in the following ways:

> the use of open questions, for example: *Show/tell me how you know? What do you find difficult? Show me what you find difficult? Tell me what you find difficult? Tell me about the properties of a square.*
> the use of closed questions, for example: *Show me a cube. Show me a square. How many corners does it have? How many sides does it have?*
> correcting teacher error;
> giving children a problem to solve related to the learning outcomes;
> working in pairs to explain a concept/skill to each other – children verbalise each other's responses and agree or disagree with the explanation then support their partner in clarifying their understanding.

You should expand the range of self-assessment strategies by using different systems. It is essential that the systems deployed provide both you and your learners with a clear understanding of current achievements and future learning needs.

Establish a purposeful and safe learning environment conducive to learning and identify opportunities for learners to learn in out-of-school contexts

Outstanding trainees will be aware of the need to engage children in outdoor learning. This should be an entitlement for all children across the early years and primary age phase. Outstanding trainees will know that outdoor learning has equal value to indoor learning and offers rich opportunities for teaching and learning in creative ways. Creative teachers will be able to teach and support learning in all areas of the curriculum through the outdoor learning environment. The opportunities are endless and limited only by your creativity and imagination.

Work as a team member and identify opportunities for working with colleagues, sharing the development of effective practice with them

As an outstanding trainee you will be aware of the value of working in collaboration with colleagues in the wider community. Now consider the range of knowledge and skills that the extended workforce within the wider community can bring to your teaching and how this can support the learning of the children. The following are examples of the range of expertise you may wish to access.

> The emergency services are usually very willing and able to support schools.
> Specialist crafts men and women or artists are usually enthused by sharing their skills with children.
> Local children's authors and poets may be willing to work with children in schools.
> Health professionals can support learning in school and may also welcome visits from schools.
> Older people within the community may enjoy sharing their experiences of significant events with children to support learning themes.
> Parents, carers and relatives may be willing to share their skills.
> Representatives from different religious and cultural backgrounds can visit the school and talk about their beliefs and lifestyles: this will provide an opportunity for children to experience and value the differences between themselves and others.

These are only suggestions and it is important that you remember that children learn best through first-hand experiences and access to secondary sources.

Professional development

Form a peer support group with other trainee teachers. Use the virtual learning environment supplied by your ITT provider and its facilities (discussion boards, instant chat, blogs) as an opportunity to exchange ideas and resources with each other. Meet with the group on a regular basis to facilitate peer learning. Trainees can participate in peer-led 'trouble shooting' seminars and each seminar could focus on a specific aspect of teaching, for example phonics, mathematics, teaching writing, planning and assessment. This will help you to realise that other trainees may be experiencing similar problems. Trainees could disseminate to their peers innovative practices in different curriculum subjects during these meetings. Present these ideas in the meeting and reflect on the ways in which they may enhance your development.

Link to research

The term 'professional learning community' has been used to describe the practice of teachers working together to improve teaching and learning. As you strive to go beyond the standards you will enhance your practice through effective collaboration with your colleagues, parents and carers, and children. This will enable you to become a more effective teacher. Evidence from America indicates that such practice has a positive impact on pupil achievement (Bryk et al., 1999). Further research in England is needed on the development and impact of professional learning communities.

Further reading

Bowkett, S. (2007) *100 Ideas for Teaching Creativity*. London: Continuum.
This text provides practical ideas for developing students' thinking skills.

Carter, J. (2002) *Just Imagine: Creative Ideas for Writing*. London: David Fulton.
This text provides practical stimuli for developing children's creativity in writing.

Green, A. (2010) *Motivating Children in the Primary Classroom: A Practical Guide for Teachers*. London: Paul Chapman.
This text focuses on a whole-school approach to motivating learners to enhance learning. It examines learning styles, accelerated learning and pupil feedback to enhance learning opportunities.

Useful websites

www.tda.gov.uk
This site provides ideas for the innovative use of ICT to support children's learning.

www.tes.co.uk/
This site provides education practitioners with specific forums which focus on a range of topics. These provide opportunities for practitioners to support one another and exchange ideas.

www.foundation-stage.info/
This site provides early years practitioners with the opportunity to communicate, and share ideas and practices.

11

Developing your own professional identity

This chapter covers

In this chapter we will consider the ways in which professional identity is shaped and how you can become a confident, reflective and outstanding teacher. Your own professional identity will develop from your own values and beliefs but will inevitably be influenced by colleagues, professional development, personal experience and a wide range of external factors. In this chapter we consider the key issues which you may need to address during your transition from trainee teacher to qualified teacher.

Developing a professional identity

As you approach your induction year you will have begun to develop an emerging sense of your own professional identity as a teacher. You will have started to develop your own beliefs and values and essentially these will inform the kind of teacher you hope to be. Wenger (1998) has emphasised that professional identities are shaped through a process of assimilation into multiple *communities of practice* and consequently identities are not stable, but fluid. This is supported by Kerby (1991) who argues that the formation of a professional identity is an ongoing process, influenced by the interpretation and reinterpretation of experiences. Coldron and Smith (1999) also support the notion of the fluidity of professional identity through engaging in professional dialogue and the sharing of ideas. They stress that rigidity and uniformity can have a detrimental impact on the development of a professional identity.

The transition from being an outstanding trainee to becoming an outstanding teacher is not automatic. Becoming an outstanding teacher will require you to:

> have an open mind;
> engage in dialogue with colleagues;
> immerse yourself in a continual process of self-reflection;
> observe other teachers and reflect on their practices;
> engage in professional development (including research).

Your professional identity is shaped by your own values and beliefs and a wide range of external influences. Throughout your career you will be challenged in a range of ways. These will include the introduction of new policy agendas and educational initiatives, working with different colleagues and adapting to the practices and policies of different schools. These influences will require you to reflect carefully on your own views and beliefs and renegotiate your professional identity. Britzman (2003) argues that the development of a professional identity is a continual 'becoming'. Consequently values and beliefs change over time and are influenced by the social contexts in which teachers work, political discourses and self-efficacy.

Britzman articulates that 'a great deal of the story of learning to teach concerns learning what not to become' (2003: 19). Throughout your professional training and subsequent career there will be copious opportunities to observe practice of others. It is too easy to be negative about other people's practice. Few lessons are perfect and observing them from a negative stance will usually result in negative judgements. Early in your careers it is likely that you will be asked to observe lessons to enhance your own professional development. Aim to identify positive aspects of a lesson and positive aspects of other people's practice. A focus for the observations may have been previously identified as a means of supporting you. Keep this central in your mind. Try to ignore the negatives and focus on the previously identified strengths of the practitioners you are observing.

Case study

Alice was in the first term of her induction year. She was teaching a challenging Year 5 class in a rural school. In an earlier observation by the head teacher it was identified that three of the children were causing some significant disruption

(Continued)

(Continued)

which was impacting negatively on the learning of others in the class. During a subsequent progress review a target was identified for Alice to develop strategies to support behaviour management.

As part of her CPD the head teacher supported Alice by arranging for her to observe the behaviour management strategies of a colleague in the school. Alice was surprised because she had already independently observed that the classroom learning environment created by the identified colleague was, in her opinion, in need of development. During the subsequent observations it became apparent that her teaching colleague had adopted very different teaching and behaviour management styles to those adopted by Alice. In Alice's classroom there were clear expectations and carefully considered reward systems. Alice focused on positive behaviour and had tried to ignore negative behaviour. She enjoyed giving children rewards but was reluctant to use sanctions. During the observations of her teaching colleague Alice realised that similar strategies to her own were used in that good behaviour was rewarded. However, there was also an emphasis on the identification of negative behaviours and strategies for dealing with this. It was noted by Alice that her colleague had an expectation that the children who had demonstrated inappropriate behaviours would themselves identify the ways in which they had behaved inappropriately as well as the impacts which these undesirable behaviours had had on others. This challenged Alice's beliefs and thinking in terms of how to manage negative behaviour. However, she acknowledged that such strategies were effective and non-confrontational. Subsequently Alice reflected on her own practices and made successful adaptations to her systems. The strategies she subsequently introduced did not entirely mirror those used by the colleague that she observed. However, she adopted many of the same principles.

Reflection

> Was it appropriate to offer Alice professional development in a classroom which, in Alice's opinion, had a poor learning environment?
> How may the identification of negative behaviours have challenged Alice's previous beliefs and values in relation to behaviour management?
> How may her initial beliefs and values have been formed?
> How did the CPD opportunity support Alice in a process of self-reflection and renegotiation of her professional identity and subsequent practice?

Tickle argues that 'we should not think of induction simply as if novices are to be socialised into some well formulated and accepted practices which exist on the other side' (2000: 1). Smith (2007) argues that first-hand experiences and observation of colleagues are powerful tools in supporting the development of professional identity. Additionally a responsibility for one's own class plays a significant contribution to the formation of professional identity (Smith, 2007). Previous personal experience and ITT have a decreasing influence in the development of professional identity compared with the influence of personal experiences (Smith, 2007). According to Smith:

> The first year working as a teacher and the intensity of that experience is seen as a powerful influence in the development of a teacher's practice and identity, or indeed whether they continue in the career. (2007: 381)

Antonek et al. (1997) emphasised that reflection is a key component of self-development as a teacher. Smith (2007) has articulated that new entrants to teaching assimilate within existing discourses related to curriculum and assessment regimes, which they readily adopt but may not critique. Dillabough (1999) offers a word of caution. She acknowledges that professional identity develops from interactions with others. She criticises the ways in which teacher competence is judged by the realisation of instrumental goals set by policy makers. Once these goals have been achieved teachers are essentially deemed as being competent (Dillabough, 1999). School development is continually influenced by ever-changing external expectations. What might these be? Although there is a need to acknowledge these, you must engage in a process of continual reflection both on a personal level and at a whole-school level to ensure that developments to your practice best suit the needs of *your* learners.

Case study

Sade was a NQT working in a good school in an urban area. As she began her first year of teaching she adopted practices conveyed to her through her ITT programme. These adhered rigidly to the recommendations of the National Strategies for teaching literacy. Within the first half of the autumn term Sade realised that this approach to planning did not fully meet the needs of the children in her class. Consequently Sade discussed her concerns with colleagues in the school, who had previously encountered similar difficulties. Through a process of collaboration, discussion and self-reflection Sade made adjustments to her planning and practices to better meet the specific needs of the children in her class.

(Continued)

(Continued)

Reflection

> In your own experience does one approach to curriculum planning, teaching and learning successfully meet the needs of all children?
> How did this experience enable Sade to renegotiate her professional identity?
> Reflect on your placement experiences to date. Identify ways in which schools and teachers have adapted current initiatives to better meet the needs of their children.

Reynolds (1996) argues that policy agendas can be persuasive, demanding and restrictive. As a reflective teacher you will need to consider whether such agendas in their entirety fully meet the needs of your learners. Teaching should not be performed by robots who blindly implement strategies and initiatives without pausing to reflect on the impact of these on learners. As a confident, educated professional you have a responsibility to critique policy agendas and curriculum initiatives and identify the ways in which you may need to adapt these for *your* school, *your* classroom and *your* children.

Developing values and beliefs

You have decided to train to become a teacher. As you embark on this journey you will already have views and beliefs shaped by family and teachers from your own schooling. You may already have a clear view of the kind of teacher you hope to be. These influences will inevitably shape your professional identity. From this point forward there will be a wide range of further influences that will impact on your values and there may be a need to redefine your professional identity.

External influences on your professional identity will begin to impact as you work with your ITT provider. You will be introduced to current government agendas and the professional standards for QTS as well as specific approaches to support planning, teaching, learning and assessment. During your professional placements you will begin to realise that schools and teachers address government policies and initiatives in a range of different ways. You will meet colleagues with differing views, values and teaching styles, which they may have developed over many years. These experiences 'in the field' will also impact on the development of your professional identity. You will need to negotiate sometimes conflicting values and beliefs and engage in a process of self-reflection. Your own professional identity will be informed by all of these sources, as well as your peers and knowledge of the kind of teacher you aspire to be and the type of teacher you feel that you ought to be.

Once you have qualified and taken on the responsibility for a class of your own you may reshape your professional identity. Smith (2007) emphasises that there has been a move away from the notion of a stable professional identity but that at specific points professional identity is more stable than at other times. Stability may be threatened through participation in different professional communities or by different government agendas. Wenger (1998) emphasises how identity is shaped by lived experience in professional communities. As you engage with different teachers in different schools your values and beliefs may be challenged. This should lead you into a process of self-reflection. This should be viewed as a positive process and one that should be ongoing throughout your professional career.

Working with colleagues in school

Engaging in dialogue with colleagues in school through informal day-to-day exchanges and professional development will inform your own professional identity. Working with colleagues in this way will encourage you to reflect on your own values, beliefs and practices. Additionally working with colleagues in teams will help you to confirm or renegotiate your professional identity. Observations of colleagues across school and feedback on your own teaching will provide useful sources of information when considering your own professional identity.

Working with other professionals

As a reflective extended professional you will work in collaboration with other professionals outside your school. This is something you may not have had the opportunity to do on your teaching placements. You may work with colleagues in clusters, on professional development courses or you may have the opportunity to work with leading teachers within your local authority. Additionally you may attend national conferences and seminars or participate in national or regional professional development courses. You also may work with colleagues from a range of different agencies.

Working with professionals outside your school may help to shape your professional identity and subsequently your practice. Working in one school for an extended period of time can become an insular experience. Dialogue with others and visits to other schools are useful and can result in you changing your own values and beliefs.

Developing partnerships with children and parents

The current policy agenda (HMSO, 2003) emphasises the importance of working in partnership with children and parents/carers. Actively seeking their perspectives about your teaching is a useful way of helping you to reflect on, and develop, your own practice. A range of mechanisms exist for collecting the views of children and parents, including the use of questionnaires and focus groups.

Professional autonomy

Teaching is a profession and consequently teachers generally have a degree of professional autonomy. During your induction career it is likely that you will need to make decisions about things that you have previously taken for granted. Hopefully you will be working in a school where you are trusted to make your own decisions about key aspects of practice. This could include:

> how to create an effective learning environment;
> how to group the learners, for example ability groups, mixed ability groups, friendship groups;
> how to organise the teaching day;
> how to teach specific learning objectives;
> approaches to assessment.

You will be supported in addressing these issues by an experienced mentor whose role it is to guide you and enhance your understanding.

To become a confident, reflective teacher you need to develop systems and approaches which best work for you and your learners. You may well find that specific approaches do not work and need to be adapted. Being trusted to determine/which approaches are successful and which are not will help you to establish your professional identity as a teacher. Having the time to trial approaches and evaluate them is a luxury that you may not have had before. It is important not to become a 'carbon copy' of your colleagues, mentors or ITT tutors. You need to engage carefully in a process of reflection and identify what your beliefs about planning, teaching, assessment and classroom management are. Once you have a clear underpinning philosophy, you will be able to plan your learning environment, your teaching and wider professional role around your own values and beliefs.

On teaching placements you have had to work within existing classroom systems and you may have had limited professional autonomy. Your transition into your induction year should provide you with an opportunity to renegotiate your professional identity. Clearly you will still need to work within school policies and systems. However, the experience you gain during your first year of teaching will undoubtedly shape your values and beliefs well into your teaching career. It is important to find a post in a school where you will be able to put your own philosophy into practice and where you will be able to enjoy some professional autonomy. Restrictive environments will be detrimental to your confidence and may constrain your growth as a teacher. Ensure that you articulate your own values and beliefs during the interview process so that your employers have a clear understanding of what you represent. Educational initiatives come and go but a well-informed philosophy of education should provide a basis for your practice throughout your career. We argue that the absence of a deep philosophy of education results in the blind implementation of policies, initiatives and approaches. We stress that confident, educated professionals engage in continuous reflection and have deep beliefs about their practice. This provides them with a basis for being outstanding teachers.

 Professional development

Engage with a new government educational initiative. Carefully consider the purpose of this initiative and the suggested approaches for implementation. Now consider the needs of children in your class. These may be wide and varying. Do the suggested approaches for implementation suitably match the needs of the learners in your class? Consider adaptations to the suggested approaches which will enable you to better facilitate learning for the children you are charged with educating.

Link to research

Lamote and Engels (2010) acknowledge the need for teachers to work collaboratively with school colleagues, external partners and parents to develop school policy and practice. This relates to Hoyle's notion of the *extended professional* (Hoyle, 1980). Jongmanns and Beijaard (1997) argue that extended professionals demonstrate greater flexibility in relation to innovations in education.

Lamote and Engels (2010) also articulate how trainee teacher professional identity is informed by the expectations of ITT providers, school-based colleagues, head teachers and the government. They state that trainee teachers are required to negotiate a range of conflicting philosophies held by colleagues in different settings and ITT providers. Consequently they have to develop a sense of how they fit in as they begin to develop their own professional identity. This is informed by the type of teacher they want to be in the future (Lamote and Engels, 2010).

According to Loughran 'it seems unlikely that the core of the personal will not impact the core of the professional' (2006: 112). This is supported by Nias (1989). Knowles (1992) and Sugrue (1997) take the stance that early childhood experiences, family and teacher role models make significant contributions to the formation of professional identities.

Further reading

Day, C. (2002) 'School reform and transitions in teacher professionalism and identity', *International Journal of Educational Research*, 37(8): 677–92.
This article provides an overview of key literature on teacher professional identity.

Boreham, N. and Gray, P. 'Professional identity of teachers in their early development'. University of Stirling. Available: www.ioe.stir.ac.uk/research/projects/epl/docs/ProfidentityNB.pdf (accessed March 2011).
This article provides a comprehensive overview of the literature related to the development of professional identity. It will be useful if you are focusing your dissertation on the development of teacher identity.

Reed, M. and Canning, N. (2009) *Reflective Practice in the Early Years*. London: Sage.
This text focuses on the importance of reflecting on your own practice in the context of the EYFS. Additionally it focuses on the issues of safeguarding and the practices of multi-agency working.

Useful websites

www.tes.co.uk/community.aspx?navcode=14
www.teacherstalk.co.uk/
www.foundation-stage.info/

These websites include forums to facilitate discussion and thus aid the sharing of advice and ideas.

List of QTS standards by chapter

Chapter 1

Q2; Q8; Q7a

Chapter 2

Q14, Q19, Q20

Chapter 3

Q1; Q10; Q14; Q15; Q19; Q22; Q25: Q26; Q27; Q28

Chapter 4

Q25a, Q25b, Q25c, Q25d

Chapter 5

Q11; Q12; Q13; Q14; Q26a; Q26b; Q27; Q28; Q29

Chapter 6

Q4; Q6; Q32; Q33

Chapter 7

Q1; Q2; Q10; Q30; Q31

Chapter 8

Q7a; Q7b

Chapter 9

Q6, Q7a, Q11, Q12, Q13, Q22, Q26ab, Q27, Q28, Q29

Chapter 10

Q5; Q6; Q7a; Q8; Q14; Q17; Q19; Q24; Q26ab, Q28; Q30; Q32

Chapter 11

Q7a; Q8

References

Alexander, R. (2010) *Children, their World, their Education: Final Report and Recommendations of the Cambridge Primary Review.* Abingdon, Oxon: Routledge.

Antonek, J. L., McCormick, D.E. and Donato, R. (1997) 'The student teacher portfolio as autobiography: developing a professional identity', *Modern Language Journal*, 81(1): 15–27.

Assessment Reform Group (2002) *Assessment for Learning: 10 Principles.* London: Institute of Education.

Beetlestone, F. (1998) *Creative Children, Imaginative Teaching.* Buckingham: Open University Press.

Black, P.J. and Wiliam, D. (1998a) 'Assessment and classroom learning', *Assessment in Education,* 5(1): 7–74.

Black, P.J. and Wiliam, D. (1998b) *Inside the Black Box.* Slough: NFER-Nelson.

Boden, M. (2001) 'Creativity and knowledge', in A. Craft, B. Jeffrey and M. Liebling (eds), *Creativity in Education.* London: Continuum. pp. 95–102.

Britzman, D. (2003) *Practice makes Practice: A Critical Study of Learning to Teach,* 2nd edn. New York: State University of New York.

Bruner, J.S. (1996) *The Culture of Education.* Cambridge, Massachusetts: Harvard University Press.

Bryk, A., Camburn, E. and Louis, K. S. (1999) 'Professional community in Chicago elementary schools: facilitating factors and organisational consequences', *Educational Administration Quarterly,* 35(supplement): 751–81.

Cheminais, R. (2006) *Every Child Matters: A Practical Guide for Teachers.* London: David Fulton.

Coldron, J. and Smith, R. (1999) 'Active location in teachers' construction of their professional identities', *Journal of Curriculum Studies,* 31(6): 711–26.

Craft, A. (2001) 'Little c Creativity', in A. Craft, B. Jeffrey and M. Liebling (eds), *Creativity in Education.* London: Continuum. pp. 45–61.

Cremin, T. (2009) 'Creative teachers and creative teaching', in A. Wilson (ed.), *Creativity in Primary Education,* 2nd edn. Exeter: Learning Matters. pp. 36–46.

Cremin, T. Burnard, P. and Craft, A. (2006) 'Pedagogies of possibility thinking', *International Journal of Thinking Skills and Creativity,* 1(2): 108–19.

Crozier, G. (1997) 'Empowering the powerful: a discussion of the interrelation of government policies and consumerism with social class factors and the impact of this upon parent interventions in their children's schooling', *British Journal of Sociology of Education,* 18(2): 187.

Crozier, G. and Davies, J. (2006) 'Family matters: a discussion of the Bangladeshi and Pakistani extended family and community in supporting the children's education', *The Sociological Review,* 54(4): 678–95.

Cullingford, C. (1991) *The Inner World of the School: Children's Ideas about School.* London: Cassell Educational.

Department for Education (DfE) (2010) *The Importance of Teaching: The School's White Paper 2010*. Norwich: The Stationary Office (TSO).

DfEE (1999) *The National Curriculum for England*. London: DFEE.

DfES (2001) *Special Educational Needs Code of Practice*. Nottingham: Department for Education and Skills.

DfES (2006) *Primary Framework for Literacy and Mathematics*. London: DfES.

DfES (2007) *Statutory Framework for the Early Years Foundation Stage: Setting the Standards for Learning, Development and Care for Children from Birth to Five*. Nottingham: DFES.

Dillabough, J.A. (1999) 'Gender, politics and conceptions of the modern teacher: women, identity and professionalism', *British Journal of Sociology of Education*, 20(3): 373–94.

Flutter, J. and Rudduck, J. (2004) *Consulting Pupils: What's in it for Schools?* London: Routledge-Falmer.

Fryer, M. (1996) *Creative Teaching and Learning*. London: Paul Chapman.

Futurelab (2006) *Learner Voice: A Handbook from Futurelab*. London: Futurelab.

Goswami, U. and Bryant, P. (2010) 'Children's cognitive development and learning', in R. Alexander (ed.), *The Cambridge Primary Review Research Surveys*. Abingdon, Oxon: Routledge. pp. 141–69.

Hayes, D. (2004) *Foundations of Primary Teaching*, 3rd edn. London: David Fulton.

Hayes, D. (2009) *Learning and Teaching in Primary Schools*. Exeter: Learning Matters.

HMSO (2003) *Every Child Matters*. Norwich: The Stationery Office.

Hoyle, E. (1980) 'Professionalism and deprofessionalism in education', in M. Atkin, E. Hoyle and J. Megarry. (eds), *World Yearbook of Education 1980: Professional Development of Teachers*. London: Kogan Page. pp. 42–54.

Hustler, D., McNamara, O., Jarvis, J., Londra, M. and Campbell, A. (2003) *Teachers' Perceptions of Continuing Professional Development,* Research report 429. London: DfES.

Hutchin, V. (2007) *Supporting Every Child's Learning across the Early Years Foundation Stage*. London: Hodder Education.

Jeffrey, B. (ed.) (2006) *Creative Learning Practices: European Experiences*. London: Tufnell Press.

Jeffrey, B. and Woods, P. (2003) *The Creative School: A Framework for Success, Quality and Effectiveness*. Abingdon: RoutledgeFalmer.

Jongmanns, C.T. and Beijaard, D. (1997) 'Professional orientation of teachers and their involvement in school policy', *Pedagogische Studien*, 74(2): 97–107.

Karpov, Y. (2005) *The Neo-Vygotskian Approach to Child Development*. Cambridge: Cambridge University Press.

Kerby, A. (1991) *Narrative and the Self*. Bloomington: Indiana University Press.

Knowles, G. (2006) 'Gifted and Talented', in G. Knowles (ed.), *Supporting Inclusive Practice*. London: David Fulton. pp. 145–68.

Knowles, J. G. (1992) 'Models for understanding pre-service and beginning teachers biographies: illustrations from case studies', in I.F. Goodson (ed.), *Studying Teachers' Lives*. London: Routledge. pp. 99–152.

Lamote, C. and Engels, N. (2010) 'The development of student teachers' professional identity', *European Journal of Teacher Education*, 33(1): 3–18.

Lareau, A. (2000) *Home Advantage: Social Class and Parental Intervention in Elementary Education*, 2nd edn. Oxford: Rowman and Littlefield publishers.

Loughran, J. (2006) *Developing a Pedagogy of Teacher Education: Understanding Teaching and Learning about Teaching.* New York: Routledge.

Malaguzzi, L. (1993) 'No way – the hundred is there', cited in C. Edwards, L. Gandini and G. Forman (eds), *The Hundred Languages of Children: The Reggio Emilia Approach to Early Childhood Education.* Norwood, N.J: Ablex.

Medwell, J. (2007) *Successful Teaching Placement: Primary and Early Years,* 2nd edn. Exeter: Learning Matters.

Meighan, R. (1977) 'The pupil as client: the learner's experience of schooling', *Educational Review,* 29(2): 123–35.

Nias, J. (1989) *Primary Teachers Talking: A Study of Teaching as Work.* London: Routledge.

Ofsted (2009) *Grade Criteria for the Inspection of Initial Teacher Education* (2008–11). London: Ofsted.

Payne, M. (2000) *Teamwork in Multiprofessional Care.* London: Palgrave.

Pollard, A. (2005) *Reflective Teaching.* London: Continuum.

Pollard, A. and Triggs, P. (2000) *Policy, Practice and Pupil Experience.* London: Continuum.

QCA (2008) *The Early Years Foundation Stage Profile Handbook.* London: QCA.

Rawlings, A. (2008) *Studying Early Years: A Guide to Work-based Learning.* Maidenhead: McGraw-Hill Education, Open University Press.

Reynolds, C. (1996) 'Cultural scripts for teachers: identities and their relation to workplace landscapes', in M. Kompf, W.R. Bond, D. Dworet and R.T. Boak (eds), *Changing Research and Practice: Teachers Professionalism, Identities and Knowledge.* London: Falmer Press. pp. 69–77.

Rudduck, J. (2006) 'The past, the papers and the project', *Educational Review,* 58(2): 131–43.

Rudduck, J., Wallace, G. and Chaplain, R. (1996) *School Improvement: What can Pupils Tell Us?* London: David Fulton.

Sammons, P., Hillman, J. and Mortimore, P. (1995) *Key Characteristics of Effective Schools.* London: Institute of Education.

Siraj-Blatchford, I., Sylva, K., Muttock, S., Gilden, R. and Bell, D. (2002) *Researching Effective Pedagogy in the Early Years.* Norwich: HMSO.

Smith, R.G. (2007) 'Developing professional identities and knowledge: becoming primary teachers', *Teachers and Teaching: Theory and Practice,* 13(4): 377–97.

Sugrue, C. (1997) 'Student teachers' lay theories and teaching identities: their implications for professional development', *European Journal of Teacher Education,* 20(3): 213–25.

Sylva, K., Melhuish, E., Sammons, P., Siraj-Blatchford, I. and Taggart, B. (2004) *The Final Report: Effective Pre-School Education.* London: Institute of Education, University of London.

Tickle, L. (2000) *Teacher Induction: The Way Ahead.* Buckingham: Open University Press.

United Nations (1990) *Convention on the Rights of the Child.* Geneva: UN General Assembly Resolution 44/25. Available: www2.ohchr.org/english/law/crc.htm (accessed March 2011).

Vygotsky, L.S. (1962) *Thought and Language.* Cambridge, MA: MIT Press.

Vygotsky, L.S. (1978) *Mind in Society.* Cambridge, MA: Harvard University Press.

Wenger, E. (1998) *Communities of Practice: Learning, Meaning and Identity.* Cambridge: Cambridge University Press.

Whitebread, D. (2003) *Teaching and Learning in the Early Years,* 2nd edn. London: RoutledgeFalmer.

Woods, P.E. (1976) 'Pupils' views of schools', *Educational Review,* 28(2): 126–37.

Woods, P. and Jeffrey, B. (1996) *Teachable Moments: The Art of Creative Teaching in Primary Schools.* Buckingham: Open University Press.

Index

Added to the page references 'g' denotes the glossary and 't' denotes a table.

ASSESSMENT FOR LEARNING IN THE EARLY YEARS FOUNDATION STAGE

Jonathan Glazzard, **Denise Chadwick** both at *University of Huddersfield*, **Anne Webster** *Teacher* and **Julie Percival** *University of Huddersfield*

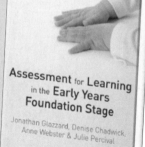

Are you struggling with the complexities of assessment? Demystifying the process of assessment for learning in the Early Years Foundation Stage (EYFS), this book explains in straightforward language how to put principles into practice.

Looking at models of assessment, the book draws heavily on examples of real assessments from practice, and the relevant theory is explained in context. Lessons from research are applied to best practice, and issues covered include:

- self-assessment and peer assessment
- collecting evidence as a basis for making judgements
- how to track the child's development in the six areas of learning
- using assessment to inform future planning
- summative assessment in the EYFS
- involving parents and carers in the assessment process
- using assessment to support children with additional needs
- moderation

Throughout the book there are plenty of practical examples from a range of early years settings, with case studies for the Birth to Five age range.

Students, teachers, teaching assistants and those working towards Early Years Professional Status (EYPS) will find this an invaluable guide.

CONTENTS

Jonathan Glazzard and Julie Percival Assessment for Learning: Theoretical Perspectives and Leading Pedagogy \ **Julie Percival** Values and Principles of Assessment in the Early Years Foundation Stage \ **Denise Chadwick and Anne Webster** Enabling Environments \ **Julie Percival** Personalized Learning: Looking at Children Holistically \ **Denise Chadwick and Anne Webster** Listening to Children and Each Other \ **Denise Chadwick and Anne Webster** Collecting Meaningful Evidence \ **Jonathan Glazzard** Summarizing Learning and Development at the End of the Early Years Foundation Stage \ **Jonathan Glazzard** Involving Parents and Carers as Partners in Assessment \ **Jonathan Glazzard** What Impacts on Children's Learning and Development? \ **Jonathan Glazzard** The Early Years Foundation Stage and beyond

2010 • 224 pages
Cloth (978-1-84920-121-6) • £60.00 / Paper (978-1-84920-122-3) • £19.99

ALSO FROM SAGE